Type & Layout

Are you communicating or

by

Colin Wheildon

With additional material by Geoffrey Heard
Foreword by David Ogilvy

Kickstarting Business Series

The Worsley Press

Parts of this book were first published as a brochure in 1984 by Newspaper Advertising Bureau of Australia as *Communicating or Just Making Pretty Shapes*.
Subsequently published with additional material by Mal Warwick as *Type & Layout: How Typography and Design can Get Your Message Across or Get in the Way*, by Strathmoor Press, Inc., Berkeley, California, USA. ISBN 0962489158

This edition, substantially revised with additional material by Geoffrey Heard, published by The Worsley Press, Hastings, Aust. ISBN 1 875750 22 3 in March 2005. Reprinted April 2007.

The Worsley Press	Distributed in the USA by:	Distributed in the UK by:
PO Bx 160	FAP Books Inc.	Eyelevel Books
MENTONE	PO Box 540	125 Christine Avenue
Victoria 3194	Gainesville FL 32602	Rushwick WORCESTER
Australia	USA	WR2 5ST, UK
info@worsleypress.com		
ABN 86 367 668 116		

© Colin Wheildon 1984, 1986, 1990, 1995, 2005
Chapters 1 and 11 and Appendices 2,3 and 4 © Geoffrey Heard, 2005

The National Library of Australia Cataloguing-in-Publication entry:

Wheildon, Colin, 1936- .

Type & layout : are you communicating or just making pretty shapes?

Bibliography.
Includes index.
ISBN 978 1 875750 22 1.
ISBN 1 875750 22 3.

1. Communicative competence. 2. Communication in marketing. 3. Graphic design (Typography). 4. Graphic arts. 5. Printing.
I. Heard, Geoffrey, 1942- . II. Ogilvy, David, 1911-1999. III. Title

BISAC classifications: BUSINESS & ECONOMICS / Advertising & Promotion BUS002000; BUSINESS & ECONOMICS / Business Communication / General BUS007000; Typography ART036000; Desktop publishing COM022000

Printed in the USA by Lightning Source Inc. and the UK by Lightning Source UK Ltd.

CONTENTS

WHAT EXPERTS SAY ...

ABOUT THIS BOOK

"The first aim of writing is to be read and understood. So, what typefaces should you use? What layouts? This priceless, highly entertaining book gives you the only cogent, logical, research into what works, what doesn't — and how 'expert' communicators often do exactly the opposite of what they should. I have cited it in seminars and correspondence for over 20 years in at least 30 countries. All other research I have seen is interesting but irrelevant as it is based on what readers *say* they like, not what actually *works*."

— Drayton Bird, *Drayton Bird Partnership, London, UK.* www.draytonbird.com

"You need this book if you use the printed word to sell, promote, or persuade! This expanded new edition of Colin Wheildon's *Type & Layout* is the indispensable guide to typography and page layout — the only book based on sound, empirical research that explains how to use type, color, and page design to get your message across to readers. You won't find Wheildon's opinions in these pages — just the facts. This book has helped me and my colleagues raise hundreds of millions of dollars."

— Mal Warwick, *Founder and Chairman, Mal Warwick & Associates, publisher of the first edition of* Type & Layout, *Berkeley, CA.*

"Design schools and colleges continue graduating students trained in 'graphic design', yet unskilled in communications. Research-based design information is largely ignored. As a result, print and web design suffers from techniques that can only be described as measurably wasteful. *Type & Layout* is a much-needed antidote for all this. It should be a prescribed text in every design school and a reference in every design studio."

—Ian McPherson, *McPherson Studio P/L, Sydney, Aust.* www.ianmcpherson.com

"I found *Type & Layout* interesting and informative on the kinds of questions I should be asking the professionals I work with. A thought provoking book."

— Peter Karpas, *Sr. Vice President, Chief Marketing & Product Management Officer, Intuit Inc., Mountain View, CA*

"If you are involved in print communication of any kind at all, go right now and get this book: *Type & Layout: Are You Communicating or Just Making Pretty Shapes?* by Colin Wheildon. It's a book about the basics of readability and design. ... Some of the principles in this book are common sense. Others will shock you. Either way, it will help you get your designers back on the job of communicating, not only creating visual art. Just get the book."

— Jeff Brooks *is a creative director at the Merkle|Domain who has worked on many major not-for-profit accounts. He was writing on* www.donorpowerblog.com — *a free service of Merkle|Domain*

"*Type & Layout* is an extremely enlightening read. ... [it] is a wonderful layout Bible... I wouldn't be without it."

— Mike Samuels, *Editor,* Mediterranean Living, *Mallorca, Spain*

"*Type & Layout* is just what many of the computer obsessed younger generation need. These days anything goes in type and layout and no-one seems to care if text can be read and comprehended easily or not. Sure, rules may be broken effectively, but Colin Wheildon's research gives us the figures that show us that we shouldn't break those rules without a very good reason."

— Rod Norwood, Director, *H W Norwood Advertising, Perth, Aust.*

"The first edition of *Type & Layout* really opened my eyes when I read it years ago. The information in it truly influences everything I design. This new edition is exciting for anyone who works with type … if they really want to communicate."

— Charles C Montgomery, *Creative design and more, Richmond, VA.*
http://home.comcast.net/~charlescmontie/index.html

"*Type & Layout* is the definitive work, based on solid research, on how best to present printed material to aid comprehension. …if you're involved in writing anything for publication, print advertising or design layout, you'll find this a gripping read. Ignore it at your peril."

— Rodney Gray, *Strategic Communication Management, UK.*

"[*Type & Layout*] gives you the skinny on what makes type work for headlines, newsletters, ads, magazines and more. This book is a valuable tool for any…marketing designer."

— Kristin Schwarz, *Graphics Program Director,*
American Writers & Artists Inc., Delray Beach, FL

"This is exactly the kind of book that is needed for people who want results from their documents and advertisements. It doesn't show art school theory; it does show real world results that have come from careful research. Anyone who is serious about creating documents or ads that really work should read and reread this book. Frequently. I do."

— Robb C. Beyer, *President, Inter/Management,*
publication researchers and designers, Houston, TX

"In 1984 when I began my business, I had Colin Wheildon's original booklet, *Communicating: or just making pretty shapes?*, tucked under my arm. Nowadays, it's hard to find a designer who knows this stuff — and none of them give a flying damn about legibility — but as an eight-time DMA Echo Winner, I can tell you that it matters very much. Using principles of this sort [as set out in *Type & Layout*], I make millions for my clients every year."

— Carol Worthington-Levy, *Direct Marketing Consultant and Partner, Creative*
Services. LENSER, San Rafael CA. www.worthington-levy.com

"*Type & Layout* should be the definitive reference for anyone involved in design, publishing and print advertising. Colin Wheildon places the emphasis where it belongs, on the comprehension of the message, and clearly shows the folly of design for its own sake. Technology has given us the ability to create virtually anything, but it doesn't bring the knowledge of how to use it effectively. Thankfully we have *Type & Layout* for that.

— Philip Hamson, *Advertising IT Liaison, Newcastle Newspapers Ltd., Aust.*

"This book should be in the toolkit of any marketer who works in the printed medium — and that is probably all of you [marketers]. It will provide an in-depth explanation and understanding of typography and layout and help you to speak knowledgeably with your graphic designers. Remember, effective marketing is not about how pretty the printed form looks — it's about how many people respond to it."

— Paul Ruzek, *Editor,* Marketing Update,
newsletter of the Australian Marketing Institute, June 2006

"Colin Wheildon's Type & Layout is compulsory reading for any marketer — indeed, for *anyone* using print media — who wants their messages read and understood. I've been using Colin Wheildon's research results as my guide for all printed material for nearly twenty years — from the time when I came across one of his early monographs on his research. In my business, I am concerned about measurable results — in the area of type and layout, Wheildon offered them and I adopted them. I have used those guidelines ever since with excellent results."

— Malcolm Auld, *Principal, Malcolm Auld Direct, The Marketing Campus,*
www.malcolmmaulddirect.com

"Every Marketing Director *must* read this important and comprehensive book before spending valuable corporate marketing dollars on advertisements, brochures and — just as important — the annual corporate report. Leaving it to the 'experts' can be dangerous to your pocketbook if these experts are clueless to the facts revealed by the studies conducted in the making of this book. You know that in this day of tight corporate budgets and cut-throat competition, you need to make every marketing dollar count. *Type & Layout* will help you do that."

— David Rumfelt, *Illustrator/Graphic Designer,*
Dave Rumfelt Illustration + Design, Toronto, Canada

"*Type and Layout: Are You Communicating or Just Making Pretty Shapes*, is the most comprehensive book I have ever read on the subject. It would be a valuable asset on the desk of any designer, beginner or advanced, whose work involves type. Thanks Colin Wheildon for doing the research."

—LaMar Bennett, *LaMarzArt, Digital Design and Fine Art, Wasilla, Alaska*

"Wise [designers] whether professional or amateur, will apply the wealth of typographical and design information in this excellent book to their printed publications to help ensure they achieve their target of communication with their audience."

— Mike Bedford, *graphic artist and educator, CA.* www.plugsnpixels.com

"I bought copies [of *Type & Layout*] for every graphic designer I know… Every designer to whom I give this book says to me 'Why didn't they teach us this stuff in design school?' *Type & Layout* is one of my most valuable books — I refer to it all the time."

— Vicky Jones, *Victoria Jones Strategic Marketing Communications, LLC, Madison WI.*

ABOUT THE PREVIOUS EDITION

"With so many typefaces and so little knowledge, college students should be considered armed and dangerous. *Type & Layout* should be required reading before students are allowed to touch a computer."

— Dennis G. Martin, Ph.D., *Professor of Communications, Brigham Young University.*

"A surprising and useful book, full of information and indispensable to anyone involved in communicating ideas through typographic means."

— Milton Glaser, *Graphic Designer, President, Milton Glaser, Inc.*

"This book has been long needed. Now we finally have the definitive guidelines that will make advertising far more effective and can save millions of dollars now wasted by poor advertising typography. Colin Wheildon has done an excellent job. He has blended solid research with the common sense that has marked his distinguished career. And he has a writing style that makes this a pleasure to read."

— Edmund C. Arnold, *Columnist and Consultant to Publications*

"For the first time, I know *why* and *what* makes me read, understand, and act when I read an ad. It is magic."

— Martin P. Levin, *Counsel, Cowan, Leibowitz & Latman; formerly President, Times-Mirror Book Company, Chairman, American Association of Publishers*

"Here is earth-shaking research which could significantly increase the effectiveness of every dollar every advertiser spends in newspapers. If readers act on the facts Colin Wheildon reveals in this book, "wealth beyond the dreams of avarice" could be theirs. If not, well, everyone's got the right to go to hell their own way. So read and remember: belief without action is worthless!"

— Reg Mowat, *Founding Executive Director, Newspaper Advertising Bureau of Australia, formerly Director, Foote Cone & Belding Australia*

"Bravissimo! *Type & Layout* may well be the most important book on print design and typography ever published. In the words of Vrest Orton, founder of The Vermont Country Store: '*If you pick up a book or a magazine and exclaim, 'Oh, isn't this beautiful type!' the designer has failed. Any type that gets in between the reader and the author is not doing its job.'* Colin Wheildon has thoroughly researched the art and science of effective print communications. Every publisher, advertiser, writer and designer must own this modern masterpiece!"

— Denison Hatch, Editor, *Target Marketing* and *Who's Mailing What!*

"Now there's nothing left to argue about! At last, conjecture, tradition, and hearsay have been replaced by the irrefutable logic of numbers and scientific survey results. Now when you break the rules, you can predict how many readers you'll lose!"

— Roger C. Parker, Author, *Looking Good in Print, The One-Minute Designer* and *Desktop Publishing* and *Design for Dummies*

"'Open Your Eyes and Listen' is the title of a seminar on type I've been giving for years. Type is speech made visible, with all the nuances, inflections, tonalities, and even dialects of the human voice. What a marvellous medium! It is one of humanity's most precious possessions — so hoorah for *Type and Layout* in crystallizing good practice in trustworthy, dependable proof. Now we can all point to chapter-and-verse. Immensely useful."

— Jan White, *Communication Design Consultant and author,* Editing by Design

"'The trouble with my students,' said the Harvard professor, 'isn't just that they don't know anything. They don't even *suspect* anything.' Colin Wheildon suspects *everything* — and he has unearthed knowledge that can give a dollars-in-your-pocket advantage to any art director or designer with the wit to take it to heart."

— Joel Raphaelson, *former Executive Creative Director, Ogilvy & Mather Chicago; co-author,* Writing That Works, *and editor,* The Unpublished David Ogilvy

"For the first time there is a body of statistically significant research to show which techniques achieve the objective of all printed material: maximum communication with readers. I convinced some of my clients to conduct tests to verify his findings in the marketplace. They quickly discovered better comprehension led to increased sales!"

— Dick Hodgson, *President, Sargeant House*

"It's reassuring to find that the typographic truths I have preached for years have a basis in hard evidence. Typography is getting increasingly chaotic. Some of it is ugly, much of it is unreadable. If Colin Wheildon's data convinces designers of a more rational typography in order to achieve comprehension, that would be welcome."

— Tom Suzuki, *Graphic Designer, Tom Suzuki, Inc.*

"This book is a must-read for any editor and designer involved with newsletters. The comprehension statistics presented in *Type & Layout* should make any designer stop and think carefully before breaking any of the rules."

— Elaine Floyd, *author,* Marketing with Newsletters *and* Advertising from the Desktop.

"Next time an art director hell-bent on 'creativity' runs your headline sideways in all caps and sets your body in white on black sans serif, fire the hotshot, and as a parting gift present him or her with Colin Wheildon's masterful book."

— Bill Jayme, *Copywriter, Jayme, Ratalahti, Inc.*

"This book is much needed by students and professionals alike. Colin Wheildon substantiates what many have long felt intuitively: that there are human factors explaining why certain type and layout approaches work better than others. The correlation between the creative and business sides of print communications explored in this book should be considered by anyone concerned about the cost-effectiveness of a publication or advertisement."

— Tony Crouch, *Director, Design and Production, University of California Press, CA.*

"Wheildon's book is refreshingly realistic — focusing on the way type works instead of just the way it looks. It scientifically proves some long-held assumptions and makes other surprising and important discoveries. Anyone who wants to get the most out of the words on their page will want this book."

— Daniel Will-Harris, *Designer and author of* TypeStyle: how to choose and use type on a personal computer.

"Wheildon's research — and this book — are an excellent antidote to desktop typesetting's license to kill communication."

— Paul Swift, *Managing Editor,* The Newsletter on Newsletters.

FIGURE 1: Doyle Dane Bernbach created this bold, imaginative ad, admired by David Ogilvy. Simple in layout and typography, it was part of a campaign which became a classic in travel advertising. The headline "screams", but since it is one word, and a familiar one at that, it works.

FOREWORD

If you write advertisements for a living, as I do, it is a matter of life and death that what you write should be read by potential customers. It's the headline and copy that do the selling.

The tragedy is that the average advertisement is read by only four per cent of people on their way through the publication it appears in. Most of the time, this is the fault of the so-called "art director" who designs advertisements. If he is an aesthete at heart — and most of them are — he doesn't care a damn whether anybody reads the words. He regards them as mere elements in his pretty design. In many cases he blows away half the readers by choosing the wrong type. But he doesn't care. He should be boiled in oil.

Fortunately, there are some art directors who do care. They do their best to design advertisements in such a way as to maximize reading. But hitherto, in making decisions about the typography and layout, they have had to rely on their guesses as to what works best. All too often they guess wrong. Thanks to Colin Wheildon, they no longer have to guess.

Some ways work better. This book reveals what they are.

No guesswork here. Only facts.

Not long ago, I read a magazine which carried 47 advertisements set in "reverse" (white copy set on a black background). These ads could not sell, because research has found that nobody reads white copy on a black background.

There are many other ways for art directors to wreck advertisements — or, for that matter, magazine or newspaper stories, annual reports, brochures, or any other sort of printed matter. This book reveals them all.

David Ogilvy
Poitou, France, September 1994

David Ogilvy died in retirement at Poitou in 1999, at the age of 88. Born in England, educated in Scotland and England, with a background in cooking, door-to-door sales, diplomacy and farming, and aged 38, Ogilvy started his own agency in New York in 1948 and built it into one of the largest in the world, Ogilvy & Mather Worldwide.

FIGURE 2: The car is red, the road is red-black, the clouds are red fringed, the sky is orange and the type (where it's not reversed out) is black. Now, what's the message? Will the shape sell more cars than the story told in the text, which certainly will not be read by most people who see the advertisement?

INTRODUCTION

What This Book Can Do for You

By Geoffrey Heard and Mal Warwick

Getting results

Why should one magazine advertisement generate thousands of inquiries while a similar ad in the same issue for a competing product fails?

How can one sales letter yield $1 million more in revenue than a similar letter, mailed at the same time to a statistically identical group of prospects?

If a newspaper editorial on a City Hall scandal sets off a public furor, why should a similar opinion piece be largely ignored?

Depending on your profession, you might explain these differences in results in a great variety of ways. For example:

- An advertising executive might compare how well each message reflects deep understanding of its readers.
- The editor might ask how well thoughts are organized and how clearly they're expressed.
- A direct marketer is likely to look first at what benefits the message offers readers.
- The designer might be most concerned with how the visual presentation looks, and in their view, strengthens (or hinders) the argument.
- A printer might examine the paper, the ink, and the quality of impression.

All these factors — and many more besides — can distinguish effective printed communications from those that fail to deliver the message. Often, there's no single "best" explanation. No communications specialist has all the answers.

In this book you will find how two apparently simple factors — typography and layout — play key roles in reading communication that specialists in other fields may find surprisingly large.

You'll benefit from this book whatever part you play in the long chain from the creation of any message to be read to its delivery to readers in printed form.

Colin Wheildon will provide you with a solid empirical basis on which to base typography and layout decisions for all kinds of print media, from flyers and letters to newspapers and books for most readers — mature readers.

In addition, we have supplemented Colin's work with information about other readers and other reading environments. Some very interesting variations show up and certainly must be taken into account.

We believe that whether you work in advertising, direct marketing, fundraising, publication design and layout, editing, or typography — or if you're a student or teacher in any of those fields — you will benefit from this book.

Pragmatic

The three editors and two publishers of *Type & Layout* all became involved with the book for one very pragmatic reason — all were attracted to the heart of it, Colin Wheildon's research into type in print media, first published in a slim monograph with the title, *Communicating or Just Making Pretty Shapes*. All three found that the effects shown translated brilliantly into practise, and having profited from those guidelines, all three had a yen to join with Colin to spread the word.

For Geoffrey Heard, contributing author, editor and desktop publisher of this edition, those parameters were the basis for publications, promotional materials, manuals and advertisements that were read, understood, and got results. For Gordon Woolf, supervising editor and publisher of this edition, Colin Wheildon's work provided confirmation of the wisdom of generations of newspaper layout artists and sub-editors, plus certainty in advising newspapers in a new era of electronic typesetting and layout. Mal Warwick, editor and publisher of the first edition of *Type & Layout*, was attracted to the work for its quantitative certainty. As a fundraiser using direct marketing methods, he could and did measure the effectiveness of his own work at every step. He put Colin Wheildon's guidelines into practise — and his monitoring showed that they *did* work and work well. He measured improved type and layout choices in big dollars.

Pleasure of design

There is no question that looking at a well-designed publication is a pleasure. There is also no question that many pages that are a pleasure to look at are *not* a pleasure to read. Design fads come and go but the basics of good design for *reading* — not necessarily *pretty* design and certainly not *noticeable* design — go on forever. The key for all three of us is that Colin Wheildon is not talking about what looks pretty, what people can read in one minute under test conditions, or whatever. He goes to the underlying reason why people write, print and display information — to convey that information to others. Then he asks whether people reading material presented in different type faces, layouts, and colors comprehend the information provided. He gave his subjects ample time to read the material, then he tested their understanding of it. The results are often surprising.

Testing versus opinions

The worlds of printing, design, editing, and advertising abound with experts who have *opinions* about typography. As a magazine and newspaper editor for more than 30 years and a typographer of long-standing, Colin Wheildon has opinions of his own — but you'll have to write to him at a Pacific Ocean beach-side seniors village in Australia to find out what those opinions are. This book is not about those *opinions*, it reports the results of nine years of hard-nosed, rigorous research. The main project involved repeated testing of more than 200 people, using methodology approved by university and industry experts. It is important to emphasize that Colin Wheildon is reporting his empirical results, not his opinions.

Both *Communicating or Just Making Pretty Shapes* and *Type & Layout* have been attacked by some reviewers, teachers and designers who, it becomes clear, have *opinions* or *tastes* which are different from Colin Wheildon's test results — but no empirical basis for them. "Helvetica is so clean, so easy to read," they might say, "and all caps really gives impact!" Fine. It might *look* clean and *look* as though it has impact, and it might be fine for one word or even a line (or some lines of sans type), but the research results show that at the end of a page, most readers either are not reading or they are not comprehending. *Not* the desired result!

One critic is Kathleen Tinkel. Writing in the *Adobe Magazine*, June/July 1995, page 36, she ripped into the previous edition of *Type & Layout* on a number of grounds, ranging from perceived inadequacy of the results to poor experimental design and inadequate reporting of the details of the experiments. It is telling that Tinkel presented no alternative data to back up her criticism, apart from vague references to "other tests" and recommended two books to be read in preference to *Type & Layout* — neither of which had any empirical basis. Better to have some faults in experimental design than to have no design and no experiment at all. Appendix 1 of this book expands on the outline of the research program and methodology employed which were given in the first edition and the monograph. It is hoped that interested scholars, including critics of Wheildon's work, can use it as a basis for designing their own studies.

It is to be hoped that they will do so without delay in the interests of furthering knowledge in this vital field. Do the research and publish your results! The world is waiting!

Unique research — well nearly!

Given the ubiquity of printing and reading, their importance in every literate culture, and the strong opinions so often expressed about choices in type and layout, it is amazing so little formal study has been carried out. Psychologists have studied the acquisition and development of reading skills, eye movements, what is attractive to the eye, and so on. There is a lot of 'folk wisdom' about, much of it very well based, some of it less so. For example, book pages tend to have page sizes, text type sizes and general layout parameters including margins, line lengths and so on within a fairly narrow range, and you will be hard-pressed to find any long, general interest book which is printed in a sans serif type face.

In the area of ease of reading and comprehension, Colin Wheildon's research, which explains why book publishers have settled on serif type faces, for example, is close to unique. In almost any other field, his ground-breaking work would have been seen as a huge opportunity for others to first, replicate his work and test his results, and second, develop new research questions which would take the work further. However, teachers and students in the design area simply have not picked up the baton — which is a pity. There is no doubt about Colin Wheildon's results — his multiple studies show that — but it is a pity this fascinating field has not been further explored.

Having said that, it is good to see some people taking a serious interest in reading using new media, particularly computer screens.

The good, the bad

A wit once said: "A computer lets you make more mistakes faster than any other invention in human history … with the possible exception of handguns and Irish whiskey."

With so much sheer typographical power at our fingertips in our desktop or laptop computers and even more available in minutes from the internet, we all have the capacity to create in short order written materials that reach new heights of unreadability!

To illustrate the kinds of things we are talking about compare the two advertisements presented in figures 3 and 4 (pp.18-19). The first is a classic in the advertising world — David Ogilvy's Rolls-Royce advertisement run in US newspapers and magazines. It is as close to exactly right as you might expect to get. And that was reflected in soaring sales.

This is the carefully considered work of the doyen of advertising practitioners of his day who was a great supporter and advocate of Colin Wheildon's work from the moment he saw it.

On the facing page, figure 4 is clearly the work of someone who has been thrown a hatful of elements and told to get them all on the page in about five minutes flat. No doubt that graphics person did their best in the limited time available under weekly magazine deadlines (the magazine's type and layout are generally very good), but the results of Colin Wheildon's research suggest that some consideration of basic elements could have made this page much more effective than it is.

Turn over the page, look at the two advertisements first, then come back to read the comments about them.

FIGURE 3 (p.18): David Ogilvy's Rolls Royce ad. ➤➤➤

- This is an example of excellent reading gravity. The eye starts by looking at the picture (color in the original) with its human faces and the subject of the advertisement, the car, strongly situated in the foreground.
- The next attraction to the eye is the headline; big enough to take the eye but not so big that it shouts at you or overwhelms the other type on the page. There is no question in your mind about where your eye goes after the picture.
- The kicker, smaller than the headline, larger than the body text, and set all italic. Many people criticize italic as being difficult to read. Wheildon's work says otherwise. Again, the eye naturally flows to it. (Setting the type centered is perhaps a little uncomfortable.)
- The body text set in an easy-to-read size in an easy-to-read three columns, with line lengths in the comfortable 35-40 character length bracket. Again, the eye has no difficulty moving from the kicker to the right place to start, it moves down and to the top left of the left-hand column — following the convention in left-to-right set text.
- The type is justified — that is, set so that both the left and right margins are even. Provided the line length and type size are appropriate, as they are here, this is achieved with only small variations in letter and word space. This makes for easy reading as the eye-brain coordination mechanism quickly figures out the predictable line lengths and adjusts eye movements accordingly.
- All type is serif for maximum readability.
- Note that the messages conveyed by the photograph and the text reinforce

The Rolls-Royce Silver Cloud—$13,995

"At 60 miles an hour the loudest noise in this new Rolls-Royce comes from the electric clock"

What <u>makes</u> Rolls-Royce the best car in the world? "There is really no magic about it—it is merely patient attention to detail," says an eminent Rolls-Royce engineer.

1. "At 60 miles an hour the loudest noise comes from the electric clock," reports the Technical Editor of THE MOTOR. Three mufflers tune out sound frequencies—acoustically.

2. Every Rolls-Royce engine is run for seven hours at full throttle before installation, and each car is test-driven for hundreds of miles over varying road surfaces.

3. The Rolls-Royce is designed as an *owner-driven* car. It is eighteen inches shorter than the largest domestic cars.

4. The car has power steering, power brakes and automatic gear-shift. It is very easy to drive and to park. No chauffeur required.

5. The finished car spends a week in the final test-shop, being fine-tuned. Here it is subjected to 98 separate ordeals. For example, the engineers use a *stethoscope* to listen for axle-whine.

6. The Rolls-Royce is guaranteed for three years. With a new network of dealers and parts-depots from Coast to Coast, service is no problem.

7. The Rolls-Royce radiator has never changed, except that when Sir Henry Royce died in 1933 the monogram RR was changed from red to black.

8. The coachwork is given five coats of primer paint, and hand rubbed between each coat, before *nine* coats of finishing paint go on.

9. By moving a switch on the steering column, you can adjust the shock-absorbers to suit road conditions.

10. A picnic table, veneered in French walnut, slides out from under the dash. Two more swing out behind the front seats.

11. You can get such optional extras as an Espresso coffee-making machine, a dictating machine, a bed, hot and cold water for washing, an electric razor or a telephone.

12. There are three separate systems of power brakes, two hydraulic and one mechanical. Damage to one will not affect the others. The Rolls-Royce is a very *safe* car—and also a very *lively* car. It cruises serenely at eighty-five. Top speed is in excess of 100 m.p.h.

13. The Bentley is made by Rolls-Royce. Except for the radiators, they are identical motor cars, manufactured by the same engineers in the same works. People who feel diffident about driving a Rolls-Royce can buy a Bentley.

PRICE. The Rolls-Royce illustrated in this advertisement – f.o.b. principal ports of entry—costs **$13,995.**

If you would like the rewarding experience of driving a Rolls-Royce or Bentley, write or telephone to one of the dealers listed on opposite page. Rolls-Royce Inc., 10 Rockefeller Plaza, New York 20, N. Y. CIrcle 5-1144.

each other. For example, it is emphasized in the text that this is a car for owner-drivers — and in the picture, the adult is sitting in the driver's seat. This is not an element of type or layout, but it is worth noting it as an indication of the level of thought that has gone into the whole advertisement. If the driver's seat were empty or worse, there was a uniformed chauffeur in the seat, it actually would act counter to the message.

Will you buy a Rolls-Royce? Who knows (check the price!) — but what is certain is that the layout of this advertisement gives you the maximum encouragement to read the text and take in the powerful selling message.

FIGURE 4 (p.19)**:** *The magazine event ad.* ◀◀◀

- Pieces of type of similar size and impact are scattered about the page. Where does the reader's eye start? Where does it go next?
- The position is further confused in the original; the "Business Week events" at the top is white reversed out of a strong red and a strong blue, embedded in a strong green band. "CEO insights" is part strong red on white and part white reversed out of the same red. That type in red and the type in blue compete strongly for the eye.
- The type that runs the full page width is black reversed out of light blue-grey. In fact, it shows here rather better than in the original, where the type is quite light. It is also too small for such line length, running something over 160 characters to the line.
- The heads beneath that block, "Forum Co-Chairs & Keynote Speakers" and "Select Featured Speakers", are too small and light to attract the eye, so the reader goes straight to the names — in bold and some of them in type larger than the heads above them — then has to return to locate the heads to attach meaning to these names.
- As the eye moves down into the list of speaker, it is in danger of being ambushed by the website URL, in blue, and the contact information, reversed out of black.
- A positive — most of the type is the same serif type, probably Caslon, which makes for good reading when laid out well.
- Compatibility between the photographs and the text? You tell me!

How we read

Colin Wheildon's research sets guidelines for print media read by mature readers — a level reached by most readers by mid-secondary (high) school age — who psychologists have shown use cues from both type and layout along with their knowledge of the language and the subject matter to see and comprehend whole phrases and even lines with quick flicks of their eyes. Psychologists have studied this in detail using movie and video cameras to capture eye movements.

Another well-researched concept in psychology also comes into play — our ability to handle only a limited number of items of information at any one time. It is one of the five finger exercises of Psychology 101 — most people can mentally handle five to seven items at once. The trick is that there is no known size limit to each of those items — you can just as easily think about an atom, a hair and a stone in your shoe as an elephant, a whale or a universe.

For mature readers grabbing whole clumps of words at a single glance, one item equals a group of words. Then they fit them automatically and unconsciously into a flexible framework constructed by their knowledge of the language and the subject for processing into concepts and clutches of concepts. Comprehension is no effort whatsoever.

Colin Wheildon's work shows how simple choices in typesetting and layout can interfere with this process right at its starting point. Even minor changes can have dramatic, sometimes counter-intuitive, outcomes. Those who disregard his research results do so at their peril!

The guidelines his research suggests hold for the majority of readers of print media — mature or fluent readers of newspapers, magazines, books and advertisements.

Other audiences, other media

There are other reading audiences and other reading media. Computer screens have burgeoned as a medium for reading (with mixed results). Research indicates that different guidelines apply for material presented on websites or otherwise intended to be read on screen. Two major factors clearly come into play: people tend to use different reading modes for screen work, and screen definition is very poor compared with print definition. Indeed, the results of Colin Wheildon's research are almost turned on their head. The same applies for materials intended for less skilled readers and those who have a vision impairment which prevents them using the usual mature reader's glance and skip method to read.

For this edition, we have sought out extra material to cover type setting and layout for people who are not fluent or mature readers, ranging from those who have not learned to read fluently to those with a vision or other impairment which affects reading.

We have sought out research in these areas; as far as possible focusing on work which has the same primary focus as Colin Wheildon's studies, measuring what our writing, type and layout are supposed to do — convey our message to our readers.

The appendices of this book provide an introduction to this area and some pointers on type and layout for them. We also briefly review psychological research that may explain some of Colin Wheildon's findings.

In a future edition, we plan to delve more deeply into these topics and to extend the range of the book to cover information presented on screen. Research is burgeoning in both fields.

A caveat

For veracity, we have used in this book real examples gleaned from newspapers, magazines, leaflets, brochures, and websites. It would have been easier to construct a parcel of examples, but it would have been even easier for critics to dismiss them as extreme, badly done, outside industry practise, etc., etc.

In examining the examples chosen and reading our comments on them, bear in mind we are measuring them against a single yardstick — comprehensibility of the written message as measured by Colin Wheildon in his research.

We are *not* saying a particular advertisement as a whole does not work well or did not succeed in meeting the criterion of selling a desired quantity of product. We are *not* saying that appropriate graphics cannot enhance the selling message or branding, even *be* the selling message or branding.

What we *are* saying is that if the meaning of the message is contained in the words and that they must be read for the message to be understood, then elements of type choice and layout can maximize or minimize the number of readers who get the message and that all those involved in production need to take these factors into account.

Example: the TRADEWINDS advertisement (figure 45, page 74). There is no doubt that the wavy lines and choice of color enhance this ad's visual appeal — but is the benefit worth the 'cost' of lost reading comprehension? The answer may be "yes" or it may be "no"; either way, it is essential that when we depart from the tried and true path, we are aware of the danger of losing readers and base our decisions on facts.

WHY THIS STUDY MATTERS

Why this study matters

By Colin Wheildon

> Typography is the art of designing a communication by using the printed word.

Typography is employed in making newspapers, magazines, books, handbills, posters, greeting and business cards, pamphlets, brochures, television graphics and, since I began my research, websites ... anything that is designed to be read.

Typography must be clear — at its best it is virtually invisible to the reader! It must follow logic, the linearity of the alphabet, and the physiology of reading. It makes no statement of its own but simply does its job of providing the best reading environment effectively and efficiently.

There is probably nothing the typographer can do to ensure a 100 per cent level of good comprehension on anything more complex than today's page of the desk calendar. It's probably true to say that there are readers who would overlook or misunderstand an article proclaiming the End of the World, but we can do things to maximize comprehension.

It is not the purpose of this book to provide enlightenment and great wisdom on graphic art. Nor is it the intention to say what is right and what is wrong with advertising, newspaper, magazine or jobbing typography.

Rather, the intention is to warn of the horrible damage some typographical elements, if used in the wrong context or thoughtlessly, can do to our creations. To put it bluntly, it's possible to blow away three-quarters of our readers simply by choosing the wrong type.

Let's set the scene by looking at figure 10a (p.34), a very simple design. We'll assume it occupies a page in a mass circulation newspaper or magazine, and that its eye-catching illustration and thought-provoking headline have attracted the attention of a million readers. We've set the body matter in an elegant serif face, say, Garamond (see figure 6, p.25).

The conditions for comprehension are excellent.

The chances are good that the message will be comprehended thoroughly by about 670,000 of those readers, two-thirds of them.

Now let's suppose that we reset the type in a sans serif face, say Helvetica, reputedly one of the more legible sans serif faces. Figure 6 (opposite) shows how this looks. The chances now are that the message will be comprehended thoroughly by only 120,000 of our readers!

So we'll revert to a roman (serif) face, but this time we'll play about a little with the headline, placing it about half way down the body matter, as in figure 10b (p.34). The number of our readers who show good comprehension of the message climbs back up to 320,000 — but we're still less than half way back to our 'square one' — the 670,000 who comprehended the message well reading the original layout.

So we'll go back to figure 10a, our first layout, but this time we'll introduce a new element. We'll put the headline back at the top but print it in a high chroma color, say hot red, or process red.

The introduction of spot color immediately boosts our potential readership to about 1.6 million — the color attracts the eye, brings readers to the advertisement! But, sadly, that very eye-catching ability works against comprehension of the text under it by constantly distracting readers. It does so to such a degree that the army who potentially could receive our message loudly and clearly is reduced to a mere division of about 272,000 — that's 400,000 fewer than we started with and only one-sixth of the number of readers we attracted to look at our ad.

And that should be enough to frighten anyone!

FIGURE 5: Typographical terminology illustrated

Term	Serif Example	Sans Serif Example
Serif/Sans Serif	This type has serifs	This has no serifs
Roman/Normal/Regular	Roman type	Normal type
Italic/Oblique	*This is italic*	*This is oblique*
Lower case	all lower case	all lower case
Capitals (Upper case)	CAPITALS	CAPITALS
Upper & lower case	Upper & lower case	Upper & lower case
Capitalize/Title	Upper and Lower Case	This Is Too
Small capitals	SMALL CAPITALS	MORE SMALL CAPS

Note on Optima and Memphis

Optima, a 'humanist' face designed in 1958 by Herman Zapf, is a hybrid, having the thick and thin strokes of a serif face, yet is sans (without) serif. Essentially it is a serif face with the serifs or terminals lopped off as shown here.

Memphis is a compromise in the other direction. It is called 'square serif' or 'slab serif', it has serifs but the strokes are of uniform thickness — more characteristic of sans serif faces.

Claims are made about the legibility and readability of these faces. They were not tested in body text sizes in this series of studies, but both was included in the headline tests. See the results in Table 7 (p.65) and figures 37 and 38 (p.66).

FIGURE 6: Just switching type face from serif to sans can result in massive differences in reader comprehension — and response — to advertisements.

A serif type, Garamond

Assume we set the body matter in the layout shown in Figure 10a (p.34) in this strong serif face, Garamond. The chances are good that the message would be comprehended thoroughly by about 670,000 readers, or slightly more than two-thirds of our million people attracted to the article.

A sans serif type, Helvetica

Assume we set the body matter in the layout shown in Figure 10a (p.34) in this frequently used sans serif type face, Helvetica. The chances now are that the message would be comprehended thoroughly by only about 120,000 readers, just a bit more than one-eighth of our million readers!

exploring
loyalty

Story and photography by Rob Woodburn

The idyllic Loyalty Islands may offer a sense of serenity

and warmth but the area has a surprisingly checquered past.

The Loyalty Islands lie east of La Grand Terre, the main island of New Caledonia. They exist on the hazy fringe of the local tourism map, yet possess a soul-soothing blend of desirable Pacific pleasures. Limpid lagoons lap against immaculate white sands, shady plantations bleed into untamed jungle-thick greenery. A tangible elasticity about each day provides the ideal formula for holiday indolence.

Ouvéa is the northernmost of the Loyalty group. It's a long, slender atoll at times barely wider than the causeway linking north and south and less than five kilometres at its widest point. The limestone interior is riddled with caves and smothered in coconut palms.

Ouvéa's western shoreline is 25 kilometres of uninterrupted white powder sand bordering clear shallow waters that deepen near fringing

reefs. However beautiful the scene may be, this particular Pacific jewel is not unblemished. Tiny Ouvéa has witnessed the worst political violence in New Caledonia. A rebellious history has effectively kept serious tourism at bay, while grim events of the past inject a cruel irony into the use of the name Loyalty Islands.

Ouvéa is a bastion of Kanak culture and tradition. Kanaky is the Melanesian name for the territory, which, in 1775, was named New Caledonia by Captain Cook. France annexed it during the 19th century and has governed New Caledonia as an overseas territory since 1956.

Melanesian Kanaks have lived here for thousands of years but today are a minority, numbering less than 44 per cent of the population. The history of Kanak-French contact has been ugly and violent. On Ouvéa, in 1988, the Kanak struggle for land

rights and independence culminated in a tragic kidnapping and hostage drama that ended in the death of 19 Ouveans and two gendarmes. Hostages abducted from the island's police station were held captive in a cave near Gosannah, in the north. The cave was eventually stormed by a large contingent of French soldiers. Two Kanak rebels were said to have been shot after surrendering.

A year later, while visiting Ouvéa, Kanak leaders Jean Marie Tjibaou and Yeiwene Yeiwene were assassinated by angry islanders outraged by what they deemed a sell-out, the signing of the Matignon Accord. This framework promised a degree of political and economic self-autonomy but with France maintaining control of foreign and military affairs, finance and immigration.

Thankfully, the political violence ended and Ouvéa has been peaceful

FIGURE 7: An elegant looking page, but this text is meant to be read. Experimental results suggest most readers will find this magazine hard going with its sans serif type set ragged right over a fairly narrow measure.

BEALUTIFUL SQUARE WHEELS

The golden rule

Fifty years ago, the eminent English typographer, Stanley Morison, gave this definition of his craft.

> "Typography is the efficient means to an essentially utilitarian, and only accidentally aesthetic, end, for the enjoyment of patterns is rarely the reader's chief aim."

That quotation is included in many text books on typography.

Usually, however, that is as far as the quotation is taken. But Morison went on to say this:

> "...any disposition of printing material which, whatever the intention, has the effect of coming between author and reader, is wrong".

This study is dedicated to exploring Morison's second tenet.

The intention is to show that certain typographical elements not only do not encourage reading, but actually discourage the reader by throwing unnecessary distractions in his or her path, interrupting reading rhythm.

The student who browses through a collection of today's magazines could be excused for thinking that typography largely had been replaced by abstract aesthetics and artistic inspiration — sometimes of doubtful taste.

Morison it appears, has become one of yesterday's men, and with him the English academic, Herbert Spencer, who said: "The true economics of printing must be measured by how much is read and understood, and not by how much is produced."

The new wave of design, in which publications and advertisements are conceived in the hope that their information content will fit neatly into the artistic design created for them, or in which they have become merely a package created on the basis of divine inspiration, is nonsensical.

Design is not, or should not be, mere decoration and abstraction, but part of the business of communication

The concern should not be for the beholder's — or creator's — eye for beauty. It should be for those who will read a publication and gain sufficient from it to want to buy it again, or the product it is advertising, or both.

The tarnished reality

But how frequently are opinions or knowledge about the invalidity of a typographic design cast aside, displaced by the view that legibility or readability isn't important if the product looks exciting?

This is absurd. A design that looks exciting but is incomprehensible is nothing more than a beautifully-painted square wheel!

Newspapers, magazines, advertisements — all printed matter — should be vehicles for transmitting ideas, and their design should be an integral part of that process, and forever under scrutiny.

Good design is a balance between function and form, and the greater of these is function. This is as true of typography as it is of an Opera House or a space shuttle. Typography fails if it allows the reader's interest to decline; it fails absolutely if it contributes to the destruction of the reader's interest.

It is easy to accept Morison's dictum that any design which comes between author and reader is wrong. What is not so easy is to identify those typographical elements which are flawed.

There is wider agreement now on some design factors, such as that serif body type and lower case headlines are easier to read than their opposites, but this agreement is little more than lip service. "The millennium is not yet upon us!" as English author and editor, Harold Evans, acerbically remarked .

Quantitative research has been hard to come by and, robbed of the benefits of empiricism, we are forced to rely on what we know 'instinctively' to be right. Regrettably, our instincts, reinforced though they may be by practical training, can lead us horribly astray.

Reading skill

The distinguished American typographer and teacher Edmund Arnold points out that reading as a learned skill has suffered much from the failure of the school system. Surveys, he says, have shown that the typical American school-leaver has a reading skill comparable to that expected of a final year primary school student. Similar problems have been reported in other English-speaking countries, including Britain, Canada, Australia and New Zealand and remedial literacy classes have become commonplace.

With this drop in reading proficiency, Arnold says, young people have become more attuned to television, which requires neither audience participation nor an attention span.

As a result, the audience for newspapers, magazines and other paper-based media, is ageing. If they are to continue to prosper, they must replace their ageing readers with converts from the television-dominated younger generation. For them, the process of reading must be as painless and physically undemanding as possible.

A would-be reader, faced with a difficult task demanding physical skill and concentration that he or she lacks, is inclined to reach for the crutch of broadcast news and ideas. And even the expert reader has a limited amount of time each day for gathering information. Therefore it is essential that typography ensures that none of this valuable time, plus the concomitant energy and concentration, is wasted.

Arnold suggests that devices which lead a reader on a wild goose chase, disturb an efficient pattern or cause the slightest measure of distress, should be eliminated.

Latin linearity & reading gravity

Arnold insists on design which pays tribute to the linearity of the Latin alphabet and the physiology of the act of reading.

When we're taught to read, we are told to start at the top left corner of the reading matter and work our way across and down, going from left to right and back again, until we reach the bottom right corner.

Arnold has devised what he calls the Gutenberg Diagram (figure 8, p.30) the principles of which, he says, all design should respect.

He says the eyes fall naturally to the top left corner, which he calls the Primary Optical Area (POA). Then, the eyes move across and down the page, obeying reading gravity, and returning after each left-to-right sweep to an Axis of Orientation.

Any design which forces the reader to work against reading gravity or fails to return him or her to a logical Axis of Orientation, tends to destroy reading rhythm and should, he asserts, be outlawed.

Where is the research?

But the question is: Is Arnold right? Where is the research that quantifies his assertions? And what of all the other maxims, axioms, and unwritten laws of printing and design that are handed down from printer to apprentice, from editor to cadet, from creative or art director to advertising trainee, like tablets of stone?

Where is the research that quantifies the supposed supremacy of serif body type over sans serif; of lower case headlines over capitals? And are

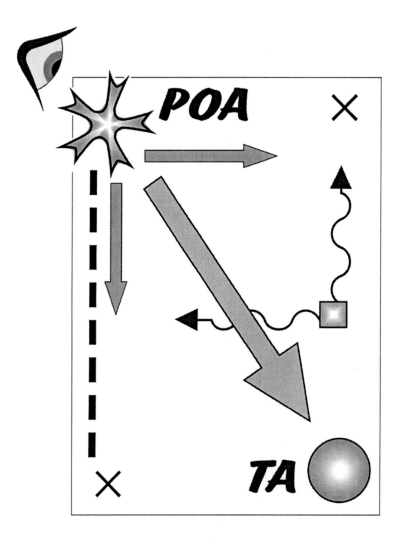

FIGURE 8: Arnold's Gutenberg Diagram charts basic reading eye movements for Latin script readers — left-right — from Primary Optical Area (POA) to Terminal Anchor (TA). The dotted vertical represents thje Axis of Orientation to which the eyes return each time they have completed reading a line. Grey arrows indicate desired eye movement directions in reading; wavy lines show 'backward' movements that the reading eye resists. "X" indicates 'fallow' corners.

headlines in spot color really productive or counter-productive, and to what extent? It is notable by its absence.

Much work has been done on research into the legibility of type faces, particularly in the early part of this century. But very little appears to have been done outside the laboratory, and more importantly, among those who buy and consume the printed word.

After a fruitless six-month search for detailed research material, I determined to conduct my own research program into the comprehensibility of reading matter, in an attempt to isolate and measure those type elements which, when used in apparently ill-considered ways, could deter, disenchant, or even antagonize the reader.

Before doing so, I sought the advice of research consultants and academics in the United States, Britain and Australia, and submitted my proposed methodology, and later the results, to them for review, comment or dissent. The consensus: that the study would be both valid and valuable for students and practitioners of typography and graphic design.

The initial program and two further programs are reported in this book. They examine a variety of elements of typographic design from Arnold's reading gravity to the perennial focuses of debate wherever and whenever users and abusers of type come together — serif versus sans serif, justified versus ragged, roman versus italics versus bold, all caps heads versus lower case heads, the use of color, line length and so on.

Texts on typography frequently allude to research into some of the elements to be examined in this research program, but, regrettably, discussion of this research is usually anecdotal rather than empirically precise.

In an attempt to bring some scientific rigor to the discussion of typography and layout, I began my research in Sydney, Australia, in 1982 and completed the major part of the program in 1986. I subsequently carried out further studies reported here, completing my work in 1990.

The speed of a Hylas is exceeded only by the speed of our development program. Leading-edge thinking inspired by modern offshore racing designs can be found throughout our line. In the 54 pictured here, a plumb bow and beamy

aft sections deliver swiftness, power and stability, while maximizing space down below. There is more than ample room for a luxurious owner's suite

A Hylas offers beamier aft sections than most other yachts (red).

aft, beautifully finished in hand-chosen woods. Offshore comfort is further enhanced by the way we build our hulls. State-of-the-art Twaron® aramid fiber construction yields bulletproof strength, for the ultimate in safety. We invite your closer inspection of the Frers designed Hylas 54 and 46. You'll find that no other yachts compete. On the water. Or on the drawing board.

Hylas Moves Ahead At A Pace Not Attained By Other Yacht Builders.

Hylas 46, 49, 54 and 54 Raised Saloon (pictured above) available.

Hylas Yachts, P.O. Box 583,
Marblehead, MA 01945
1-800-875-5114

Built by Queen Long Marine Co. Ltd.

OOPS! GRAVITY WORKS!

The perils of ignoring gravity

The first precept examined was the positional relationship of headlines to body matter: whether the irregular placement of headlines could cause a break in reading rhythm strong enough to affect the reader's concentration.

The layout in figure 10a (p.34) complies with Arnold's Gutenberg Diagram. It was contrasted with a layout, shown as figure 10b (p.34) which defies the principles he has enunciated.

On any page where there is writing or printing, the starting point is the upper left corner. Here the eye, trained from babyhood, enters a page, and here it must be caught by an attention compeller. When the eye reaches the lower right corner, after scanning across and down progressively, the reading task is finished. Reading gravity doesn't follow a straight line; it moves to right and left, and has to be lured to what are called the fallow corners by optical magnets, usually illustrations.

The eye does not willingly go against reading gravity, with the obvious exception that, having read a line of type or writing, it uses that line as a guide as it jumps back and drops down to the next line.

Arnold calls the point to which the eye returns the Axis of Orientation (see Figure 8, p.30). Any variation from this causes an interruption to reading rhythm. This characteristic is used, as here, to mark paragraphs. Arnold says that if this axis is altered by typographical means, the eye is likely to rebel, and a reader may become an ex-reader.

In figure 10a, it will be seen that the eye falls naturally to the headline, the Primary Optical Axis, and the principle of the Axis of Orientation being obeyed, would fall to the introduction, then follow naturally the flow of the body type. The two pieces of halftone illustration act as magnets to the fallow corners, and the sign-off logotype acts as the Terminal Anchor.

FIGURE 9 (left): *Gravity defied. The headline's position in the depths of the picture leads the reader straight to the logo and contact information. The end! How many people will find their way back up to the beginning of the text? The body type is a well chosen serif design but set with an exaggerated leading (interlinear spacing) which is a further hurdle to reading and comprehension.*

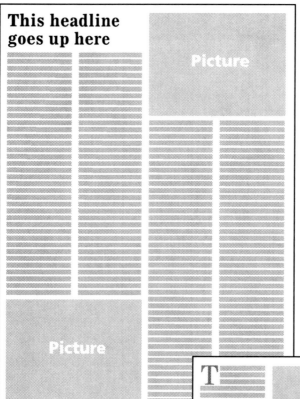

FIGURE 10: Experimental layouts, newspaper/formal. Note how moderate the anti-gravity test layout is compared with the real examples, figure 2 (p.12), figure 9 (p.32), figure 13 (pp.38-39) and figure 24 (p.52). How much greater would the loss of reader comprehension be if more extreme anti-gravity layouts were tested?

10a (left): A page constructed along lines suggested by the Gutenberg diagram.

10b (right): Simply moving the headline and one illustration to accommodate it slashes good comprehension of the material by half.

In figure 10b, instead of being attracted by the headline to the top left corner, the eyes are attracted by the headline to a point below the upper illustration. Having read the headline, the eyes want to observe the principles of reading gravity and the Axis of Orientation, and fall to the small leg of type in the second column. This obviously will make little or no sense.

The eye then is forced to make the journey against reading gravity to the Primary Optical Area to begin the article. The reading rhythm has been destroyed, and, as the research program shows, considerable damage may have been done to the reader's comprehension of the article.

Newspaper or formal layouts

In the research program, the readers were subjected to an equal mix of both types of layout. Headlines in each instance were 42 point Helvetica bold lower case, two decks (lines), set over 27 picas (4½ inches; 11.5 centimeters); body type was 8/9 point Corona lower case over 12½ picas (two inches; five centimeters); illustrations and captions were of identical size in each layout. Layouts were four columns, 12½ picas wide (2 inches; 5 centimeters) and 30 centimeters (12 inches) deep — a total body type area, pictures excluded, of about 65 column/centimeters (26 column/inches).

The types chosen were selected because of their potentially high legibility. They were optically rather than geometrically drawn, had easily discernible differences between letters, and had greater x-heights than alternatives.

The layout in figure 10b contained one design element not used in

FIGURE 11: *Sample of newspaper-style type used in the formal layout (figure 10).*

Headlines like this

Body copy in articles used in the research looked a lot like this. This type is Corona — a robust newspaper or magazine text face. And this text is set 8 on 9 point over 12½ picas, as was the text in the research. Body copy in articles used in the research looked like this.

figure 10a. In an attempt to induce readers to make the jump against reading gravity from the second deck of the headline to the introduction paragraph, a drop initial was used. In figure 10a, a drop initial was not used because of the likelihood that it would clash with the headline.

Participants were asked to read two kinds of texts, texts of direct interest to them and texts of limited interest. *When this methodology was used*, the results were highly consistent — the levels of comprehension of articles of direct interest were about five percentage points above the average, and those of specific or limited interest, within five percentage points below the average. This, with one statistically insignificant variation, was so for all tests in the program.

Table 1 (below) shows the *averages* for tests across direct and limited interest articles. The comparison between formal (newspaper) and free (magazine) layouts (table 2, p.41) uses only the higher 'direct interest' results: good, 72 per cent, fair, 20 per cent and poor, 8 per cent.

Results

Table 1: Comprehension of text with good reading gravity is double that with poor reading gravity. Percentage of readers' achievement as an average of all tests.

Comprehension level	Good	Fair	Poor
With reading gravity	67	19	14
Disregarding reading gravity	32	30	38

Following the formal questions readers were invited to comment on what they had read, and on the way it was presented.

None of those who registered high comprehension commented on the design. However, many who scored poorly with figure 10b layouts said they found they were conscious of having to find their way to the beginning of the story — the eyes fell naturally to the leg of type in column two, instead of making the journey back to the top of column one. Yet those same people scored well in comprehension when reading similar articles in the figure 10a layouts with good reading gravity.

Of those who scored "poor", a high proportion answered correctly the questions linked to the early part of the articles, then failed to score again. Similarly, those who scored "fair" generally achieved their correct answers among the four to six questions relating to the early part of articles, then apparently failed to read on, or did so in a cursory manner.

This supports the contention that readers who are faced with a journey

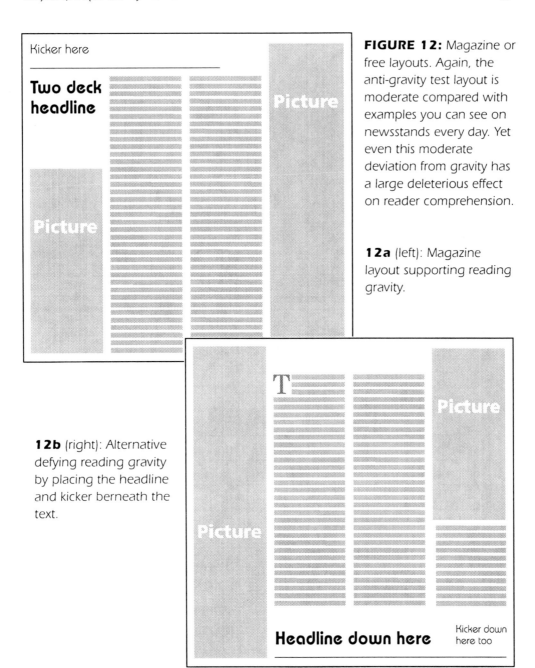

FIGURE 12: Magazine or free layouts. Again, the anti-gravity test layout is moderate compared with examples you can see on newsstands every day. Yet even this moderate deviation from gravity has a large deleterious effect on reader comprehension.

12a (left): Magazine layout supporting reading gravity.

12b (right): Alternative defying reading gravity by placing the headline and kicker berneath the text.

FIGURE 13 (pp.38-39): Oh no! Where does my eye go? A classic case of anti-gravity — with an unhealthy leavening of other anti-reader devices. Most of the problems here could have been resolved by switching the two pages and flopping the illustration on the left-hand page so it could serve the same purpose but on the right-hand side. ➤➤➤➤

The kicker — the real point where the reader's eye needs to go after the headline. But the eye is diverted from it by the drop cap below.

The giant drop cap is often a designer's tacit admission that all is not well with reading gravity.

Black text running over bright blue. Tough reading.

Catch the line beginnings if you can! Text layout changes to ragged left, with its inconsistent line beginnings buried in the illustration's mainly blue and black colors. Reading confusion!

Very narrow column of type and very large word spaces are further impediments to reading.

Once upon a time, a favourite of Luna Park habitues was to hurl crockery at an effigy of Kaiser Wilhelm. Now, 90 years on, Luna Park hurls its patrons around in a stomach-churning attempt to compete with the high-tech big boys. Cartoonist **George Haddon** and writer **Lawrence Money** take a walk through "Mr Moon" to get the inside story on this St Kilda icon

A Scenic Railway scream is pretty much the same as a powerful drug, sort of, in that, like a passing train while, it is accompanied by a roar of wheels and machinery, and it drops a semi-tone as it hurtles by. Above Luna Park's "Mr Moon", the giant mouth that swallows all who enter, you could once hear two-breed screams from the adrenaline tragics aboard the Scenic Railway and the higher (and scarier) Big Dipper. But the Dipper and its track-on-stilts is just a memory these days, along with that weary little monarch whose taped laugh crackled non-stop from a window in the vanished Giggle Palace (it burnt down 19 years ago, presumably barbecuing the king).

Ah yes, many a thrill has come and gone at this field of screams. In 1912, when it opened on the site of a pioneer fort called Dreamland, Great Grandma would have gasped at Miss Thelin, a Swedish lass who dived from a 15m tower, with clothes ablaze, into a pool of fiery water.

Great Grandpop may have had his laugh during the war years, hurling crockery at an effigy of Kaiser Wilhelm down in Show Alley. It was a semi-circus, with performing animals and a troop of midgets. Within two years the place was drawing 8000-10,000 people each Saturday night.

Now it is a different story. Walk in under those maxi-molars and you find a Melbourne icon stuck between the giggling past and the high-tech future. Sydney spent $100 million refitting its Luna Park, which reopened two months ago, but the Mouth from the South, despite $10 million spent by owners BCR, has remained in limbo. BCR put the park up for

At first glance, gravity looks good! The eye hits first on the eyes in the face in the bright illustration, then goes around to the headline (all caps but only four words), the byline (set right; why?), then to the top of the first column of the body text and... **WHAT !?!?**

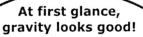

MOUTH FROM THE SOUTH
by George & *Mister Money*

SHOCK, HORROR !!! We are in the middle of a sentence! Gravity is dead and we readers, are lost!

sale early this year but hopeful reports that new owners would restore the old favourites are "poetic licence," BCR boss Ron Bassett tells us. Tick off those vanished attractions: the River Caves, the long ... inside the Giggle Palace, ...y mirrors, th... ...in, ... arcade, ... stuck ... like a ... ble is ... of ...d and... ...vorld ...sed the ... instead ...ne Rotor you ...w find the Mad M... ... heavy-duty vertigo... ...ned Enterprise. ... ...as to assign cartoonist George to test-pilot

the ... ...prise but the dear fellow ...cli...d, explaining that the m... ...ics of the device (an "inclined ...lar motion and continual ...ver-sion of riders", according to the warning sign) would clog the ink in his pen.

There have always been two types of patrons of Luna Park: the gentle River Caves type and the thrill-seeking Big Dips. For River folk, the perennial clown heads are a safe bet. They are still oscillating back and forth like the front row at Rod Laver Arena during the Open. How many million ping pong balls have gone down those throats?

Nearby is the park's grand old masterpiece: the giant carousel, restored to its kaleidoscopic glory in 1999. BCR ...ent $2.2 million fixing up ...is c... ...uty only to se... ...e Friends of L... ...rk, ...h lobbied for the project, enjoy most of the limelight. "They didn't put in a penny," growls Ron, hinting that relations are not entirely cordial.

Anyhow, the carousel came up a treat and, during the restoration, workers levered off a board which had covered the maker's name for over 80 years: the Philadelphia Toboggan Company.

Man, that's some toboggan!

against reading gravity unconsciously find the effort demanding and do not read an article with the same easy concentration as do those whose reading rhythm has not been disturbed.

Magazine or free layouts

At the conclusion of these tests using formal layouts such as might be used in newspapers, a supplementary test was made using free layouts, as might be used in magazines.

The body matter was set in 9/10 point Corona Roman over 15 picas, and a more leisurely headline type, 72 point Bauhaus Bold lower case with a kicker line of 24 point Bauhaus Medium lower case, was used.

The layouts are shown as figure 12 (p.37), 12a, a design complying with the principles of reading gravity, and 12b, a design ignoring those principles. In figure 12b, a drop initial was again used in an attempt to draw the reader's attention from the headline to the introductory paragraph.

Only one type of article, general interest, was used in this test, as opposed to the two in the previous test. The articles had the common theme of domestic tourism, a topic shown in magazine reader attitude surveys to have wide appeal.

FIGURE 14: *Magazine layout and type sample.*

Kicker

Head

Body matter in magazine articles used in the research looked a lot like this, it was set in 9 on 10 point Corona Roman, as this is. Body matter in magazine articles used in the research looked a lot like this, it was set in 9 on 10 point Corona Roman, as this is. Body matter in magazine articles used in the research looked a lot like this, it was set in 9 on 10 point Corona Roman, as this is.

Results

The results showed a marked similarity to the results achieved in that part of the major test employing articles of direct interest.

Remember that the layouts used in figures 10b and 12b which disregarded reading gravity, were given a typographical crutch in the shape of a drop initial on the introductory paragraph. The point having been made that even with a crutch these layouts failed in their objective, it was not considered necessary to calculate how much further they might have failed with this crutch removed.

The comparison between these results and the results of the formal layout relating to articles of direct interest is shown in table 2.

Table 2: Comprehension level of text in both formal and free layouts falls by half when readers are forced to go against reading gravity.

Comprehension level	Good	Fair	Poor
With reading gravity — figures 10a & 12a			
Formal layout (n'paper)	72	20	8
Free layout (magazine)	73	21	6
Without reading gravity — figures 10b & 12b			
Formal layout (n'paper)	34	31	35
Free layout (magazine)	37	31	32

The conclusion to be drawn must be that designs which conform to normal reading practise — reading gravity — are largely acceptable to readers; those that don't conform run the risk of going largely unread.

The advertisement shown in figure 9 (p.32) was in a glossy magazine. The danger is that readers' eyes will be drawn to the headline, a false Primary Optical Area, then will fall naturally to the copy beneath. When this doesn't make sense, they are likely to give up and turn the page. Even if they fight against gravity, the research results suggest many readers will rapidly lose interest anyway. How many possible sales will be lost?

Figure 13 (pp.38-39) is another example. The headline attracts the eye, which then falls to the text immediately below in the first column. This makes no sense, so off go the readers' eyes desperately seeking the starting point. How many readers would make the effort? And if they did, how many would read more than a few lines before they gave up?

What of the obstacle course for the reader provided in figure 2 (p.12)? Was the intention to illustrate the nature of the terrain as described in the copy? In addition to the headline being at the bottom of the text, the copy is near impossible to read. Whether the words in this advertisement succeeded in communicating their message is highly questionable.

Another example is figure 25 (p.52) with the headline slicing the body text in two. Readers automatically go to the top of the left-hand column under the headline, find it makes no sense, and, it is hoped, find their way back to the top left of the page. They read down, then where do they go? Jump the headline to continue down that leg or go up to the start of the next leg? No wonder readers lose patience.

In contrast, the magazine page shown in figure 16 (opposite) provides readers with a clear path complying with reading gravity.

So having determined that the simple design style, shown in figure 10a, was acceptable to most readers, I retained it for the remainder of the program, and discarded figure 10b.

Conclusion

The results shown in tables 1 and 2 (pages 36 and 41) and in figure 15 (below) show that there can be no question: the influence of reading gravity is substantial. More than twice as many readers will readily understand text presented in a layout complying with the principles of reading gravity than one defying reading gravity, while a layout defying gravity will lose more than a third of readers to poor comprehension.

FIGURE 15: (From table 1.) The effect of reading gravity on comprehension of text. Anti-gravity halves the number of readers who achieve good comprehension and more than doubles the number lost to poor comprehension. This is disastrous when good comprehension equals the full sell of an advertisement and poor comprehension means loss of the reader before closing the sale really begins.

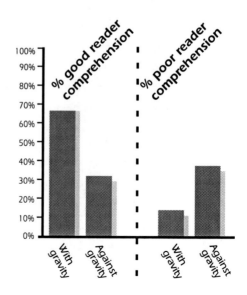

FIGURE 16: Easy reading from THE SPECTATOR in the UK. The huge drop cap and position of the kicker are a little fiddly, though. Giant drop caps are the design fad-of-choice from time to time.

FINE ARTS SPECIAL

The rights and wrongs of conquest

'Give us back our marbles' is the cry. Passionate demands are made for the return of famous works of ancient sculpture. In response, there is equally heated resistance. Sending them back would be an offence against civilisation, it would break up a great collection. Only in a mighty museum in a sophisticated metropolis can such works truly make sense. Their surrender would be an aesthetic tragedy and — worse — national humiliation. Of course, it all sounds extremely, indeed wearyingly, familiar.

But this is not another account of the eternal dispute about the Elgin (or, if you prefer, Parthenon) Marbles, but a résumé of the debates that preceded the breaking-up of the Musée Napoléon in 1815. It's just that the arguments deployed were almost exactly the same — and, ominously for the BM and its supporters, 191 years ago it was the let's-not-lose-our-marbles brigade who lost.

Now almost forgotten, the Musée Napoléon briefly contained almost all the

France gave back artefacts looted by Napoleon. So what's different today? asks Martin Gayford

Horse of St Mark's by Charles Freeman (Little, Brown, £16.99).

In fact, that well-known chariot team was just about the only notable work not put in the Louvre, where the Emperor's museum was housed. The four horses were placed on top of the Arc de Triomphe du Carrousel. But the Apollo Belvedere from the Vatican, Rubens's 'Descent From the Cross' removed from Antwerp Cathedral, Raphael's 'St Cecilia', the 'Venus de'Medici' and all the rest were in the Louvre. And that, in the general French view, was where they ought to remain.

All this loot had been removed from its owners by right of conquest. 'The fate of products of genius,' as an official declaration on the subject put it, 'is to belong to the people who shine successively on earth by arms and by wisdom, and to follow always the wagons of the victors.' Furthermore, obviously, Paris — being the most advanced spot on the globe — was

the natural home of the world's finest works of art.

'The French Republic, by its strength, superiority of its enlightenment and its artists, is the only country in the world which can give a safe home to these masterpieces.' (Compare the claim made on behalf of the BM over the last century and more: only in Bloomsbury can such treasures remain secure.) But even after Gallic arms had ceased to conquer all, it was still felt — especially in Paris — that all this stuff was really seen to best advantage beside the Seine.

This was partly a reflection of the belief — universal among curators — that once an item has entered a collection it must never, ever leave. The collection itself becomes a unity which it is rank philistinism to break up. Within it, the works can be compared, one with another across centuries and cultures, in a way they never could be it sent back to their original homes. This was very much the view of the director of the Musée Napoléon, Vivant Denon (as it is of the BM staff and their proponents).

After Napoleon's first surrender, and exile to Elba, the victorious allies were inclined to take the same view. Let the French keep what they'd got. This was partly on the can-of-worms principle: in a similar way it is argued these days that it

FIGURE 17: Practically no gravity. Heads and pull-outs in every color of the rainbow. Plenty of words, but no clear path for the eye to follow. Not a great read, but it may function perfectly well with its intended audience.

TYPEFACES

Emotion and legibility are two issues at play when selecting typefaces for any marketing communication. dm asked some fonts of knowledge for their take on typefaces

1 There are no right or wrong typefaces, only effective and ineffective ones. Just as people tend to form an opinion of you by your appearance, the first impression of type is also important. If you want your business to be taken seriously, you need to choose a font(s) that reflects this. Don't use a casual or script font when a credible, more traditional typeface would be more appropriate. At the same time, don't use Times New Roman or Arial because everyone else does. **PW**

2 Fonts, like people, come in all shapes and sizes – they have distinct personalities. The right typeface can reinforce your message, whereas the wrong one can detract from your intended meaning and adversely influence your audience's opinion of you and your ideas. Choose an appropriate font for your graphic material by asking, what is the tone of this project? **PW**

Fun, happy, credible, serious, professional or exciting? Choose a font that reflects you and your messages.

Think about what font best reflects the content. If you're talking about insurance, you want a font that is open, easy to read and reflects the credibility of your business. A leaning font with a cute feel is going to contradict this.

3 What font is appropriate for this medium? Choose a font that works effectively in the medium you are using for your communication. Some fonts render well onscreen while others are better for printed material.

Do we have a corporate font? If you have a corporate font, use it. Ask your graphic design department or your designer what it is and make sure it is installed on your computer. Reputable designers spend considerable time and use proven methodology to select appropriate business fonts. Stick to their advice. **PW**

4 Flexibility from your typeface is important if you plan to use a consistent font throughout above-the-line and below-the-line executions. It needs to work as well in a DM piece as it does on a TVC end screen or outdoor super site. The typeface represents a tone of voice where no voice over is used – your font selection should give the text a tone that's relevant to the content and audience. For example, our current campaign to attract blood donors relies on the 'hard facts' of blood donation (80% of Australians will need blood during their lifetimes, yet less than 3% donate blood). To support this feeling of clinical, hard facts, a bold 'matter of fact' font is used. A more relaxed, emotive campaign would call for a warmer font. **AH**

5 Fonts can scream or they can whisper. Typefaces should be chosen based on the idea you are trying to convey – they are a complement to your thoughts. Rules are sometimes meant to be broken, but with typography there's an art to the craft and when the fundamentals are ignored– perhaps your font is fighting with the original idea – your message will fail. **DM**

6 For messages that need to have impact, use staggered text in a variety of sizes and weights, particularly in brochures to customers. OPSM sets the first paragraph in a heavier weighted font, which helps pull the reader into the rest of the information. **KH**

7 For body type in DM it is essential to choose a serif font. Comprehension levels for sans serif are far lower than for serif (one theory is that serif typefaces lead the reader's eyes from one letter to the next). However, even with serif, comprehension levels are nowhere near as high as you might expect. **FC**

8 The biggest rule about type in DM is that you shouldn't use 'reversed out' type. Numerous tests have proved that 'reversed out' is harder to read. It may be okay for a short heading but for body copy it is out. **FC**

9 Typography is the joint responsibility of the writer and the art director. To create readable copy, you must understand how your copy relates to the page. The writer must continually work with the art director to ensure comprehension as well as visual impact. **JS**

10 There are lots of theories about the advantages or disadvantages of certain typefaces. Most of these really relate to current trends more than any scientific fact. Pick up an award annual in any particular year and you will find that ads tend to have a sameness to their look. Franklin Gothic Bold Condensed had a good run for a while. One thing I'm a stickler for in DM is that type is clean and easy to read. It needs space to breathe on the page – if it looks too hard to read it generally will be. Our job is to make a proposition not just compelling, but easy to digest. By all means use different family members of the same font, but more than two fonts on a page usually starts being a hazard. **SC**
dm

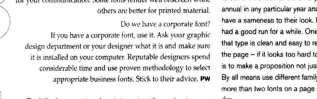
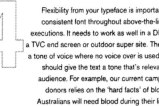

Top 10 panel

- Adam Hodge, national marketing and communications coordinator, Australian Red Cross Blood Service (AH)
- Darren Martin, senior art director, Clemenger Proximity (DM)
- Frank Chamberlain, director, Action Words (FC)
- Jeff Sanders, managing director, Rapp Collins (JS)
- Krista Hoey, group communications manager, OPSM (KH)
- Paul Wilson, creative director, Hot Chilli (PW)
- Stuart Clark, national creative director, TEQUILA\DM (SC)

BODY TYPE

There are three recurring arguments about body type: the choice between serif and sans serif faces; the use of italics and bold type as substitutes for roman/regular; and whether type should be set ragged or justified.

Serif or sans serif?

On this question — which is easier to read: serif or sans serif body type — there appears to be complete polarization of thought.

There are few major newspapers in the English-speaking world today which use sans serif type for the body text. Conversely, many major magazines choose sans serif.

Serif faces have long been regarded as highly readable. One theory was that the serifs acted as tram lines, keeping the eyes on target. Another was that the modulated thick and thin strokes of serif types provided greater opportunity for individual letters, and hence words, to be distinguished and read.

Figure 19 (below) contrasts a serif type, with its thick and thin strokes and terminal serifs, with a sans serif face with its uniform strokes and absence of serifs.

FIGURE 19: A serif typeface — Garamond (top). A sans serif — Futura (below).

abcdefghijklmnopqrstuvwxyz
ABCDEFGHIJKLMNOPQRSTUVWXYZ
1234567890_+,/!@#$%^&*()_+<>?

abcdefghijklmnopqrstuvwxyz
ABCDEFGHIJKLMNOPQRSTUVWXYZ
1234567890_+,/!@#$%^&*()_+<>?

FIGURE 18 (left): Words about type. The page looks dramatic, but more than half of the article is set ragged left, the rest ragged right, much of it in sans serif and the gray numbers interfere with reading. In #10, the lack of science behind many type decisions is noted. Colin Wheildon's research presents the facts.

Not all serif faces, nor all sans serif faces, share similar characteristics. Fat Face, for example, is quite different in many respects from Times New Roman, although both are serif types; Univers, an optically-designed face with considerable variation in the stroke thickness of individual letters, is different from the geometric, theoretical Futura (figure 19, p.45), with its identical thickness in strokes and bowls. The appearance alone of Fat Face and Futura ought to shout a warning about their readability as body types, but nevertheless Futura enjoys a vogue with designers from time to time. In this study, the terms serif and sans serif are taken to refer to those more moderate examples of their styles, which are generally used in text by newspapers, magazines and advertising agencies.

FIGURE 20: *Two serif and two sans serif faces indicate the range of variations among type faces. Note the size differences, despite the fact that they are all set to the same nominal size of 14 points.*

This sentence is set in New Yorker.
This sentence is set in a Fat Face.
This sentence is set in Optima.
This sentence is set in Skia.

Clean, uncluttered, attractive ... but comprehensible?

In research collated by the British Medical Council in 1926, it was asserted that the absence of serifs in sans serif body type permitted what the council referred to as irradiation, an optical effect in which space between lines of type intruded into the letters, setting up a form of light vibration, which militated against comfortable reading. Serifs, the research said, prevented this irradiation; thus serif types were easier to read.

Some magazine editors, art directors and creatives argue that sans serif should be used as body type because it is clean, uncluttered and attractive.

And so it is. But they also argue that any difficulties with reading and comprehensibility — should they exist — will pass, as people become more and more accustomed to seeing and reading sans serif. People will grow to live with it, and it will soon become comprehensible to all, and all will eventually love it, they say.

But regardless of the validity or otherwise of this argument, doesn't it miss the point? All those involved in the production of all printed matter, writing and laying out advertisements, newsletters, sales letters, brochures, magazines, newspapers and books, need to ask themselves what they are supposed to be doing — what they are *paid* to do. Surely that real task is to communicate *now*, to attract the reader's eye and be read, understood and acted on right this minute, not to attempt to teach people to read fad-of-the-day alternative type faces.

To communicate now, we must use the type faces which are proven to result in the best comprehension.

In the tests on the comprehensibility of serif body matter versus sans serif, the same procedure was used as for the previous series of tests. Body type was 8 point Corona on a 9 point body for the serif layouts, and 8 point Helvetica on a 9 point body for the sans serif layouts.

Results

TABLE 3: Comprehension levels — percentages of 224 participants. Five times more readers achieve good comprehension with serif type than with sans serif.

Comprehension level	Good	Fair	Poor
Serif body type	67	19	14
Sans serif type	12	23	65

FIGURE 21: Charting only the "good" and "poor" numbers dramatizes the huge difference a shift from serif to sans serif body text makes to good comprehension of printed material. With san serif type, two-thirds of readers are effectively lost.

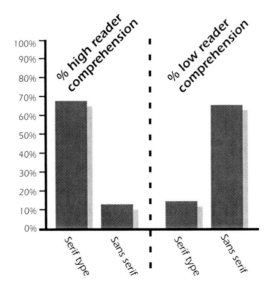

Comments

Comments made by readers who showed poor comprehension of articles set in sans serif had a common theme — the difficulty in holding concentration.

A summary of the comments offered by one group of 112 readers who read an article of direct interest follows. Sixty-seven of them showed poor comprehension. Negative comments included (some made more than one comment):

- Fifty-three complained strongly about the difficulty of reading.
- Eleven said the task caused them physical discomfort (eye tiredness).
- Thirty-two said the type was merely hard to read.
- Ten said they found they had to backtrack continually to try to maintain concentration.
- Five said when they had to backtrack to recall points made in the article they gave up trying to concentrate.
- Twenty-two said they had difficulty in focussing on the type after having read a dozen or so lines.

Yet when this same group was asked immediately afterwards to read another article with a domestic theme, but set in Corona, they reported no physical difficulties, and no necessity to recapitulate to maintain concentration.

Conclusion

The conclusion must be that body type must be set in serif type if the designer intends it to be read and understood. More than five times as many readers are likely to show good comprehension when a serif body type is used instead of a sans serif body type.

Bold & italics

Printed in bold

Bolding text is a common way of emphasizing text within body matter, breaking up long text to make the page more visually appealing or drawing attention to special material, such as a side bar or subsidiary article. It is also used for long text printed over a tint or photograph to make the text stand out better.

A series of tests was conducted with text printed in bold type.

Bolding text certainly has the effects touted for it; it catches the reader's say Tenet did not resist strongly enough the alleged pressure to provide the White House with pretexts it needed for an invasion of Iraq that it had already decided upon. It all came to a head in April with the publication of Bob Woodward's book *Plan of Attack*, which includes a scene in which Tenet lays out for the President the evidence that Saddam possessed chemical and biological weapons. "George, how confident are you?" Bush asked Tenet. "Don't worry," he answered. "It's a slam dunk."

More than a year—but no WMDs—later, those words have returned to slam-dunk Tenet. It doesn't help that the controversies over Iraq and 9/11 follow on intelligence failures stretching back almost to the beginning of Tenet's reign. In his seven years as director of Central Intelligence—only the legendary Allen Dulles served longer—Tenet revived morale at an agency devastated by post–cold war budget cuts and a sharp drop in recruitment. But he also presided over blunders that included the agency's failure to foresee in 1998 that India would test an atomic device, and the mistaken identification one year later of the Chinese embassy in Belgrade as a bombing target, an error that resulted in the deaths of three embassy staff members. The CIA also failed to foresee al-Qaeda's dual bombing in 1998 of the U.S. embassies in Tanzania and Kenya or its attack on the U.S.S. *Cole* two years later.

Once Tenet steps down, his acting successor will be Deputy Director of Intelligence John McLaughlin, a career analyst. It is a cliché to call McLaughlin unassuming and modest; it is more telling to describe him as deeply analytical and alert to the ambiguities of his trade. An amateur magician, he is especially adept at sleight of hand, a skill that helped win him the nickname "Merlin."

McLaughlin may need his magic powers, for one of his first challenges will be to defend the agency against attempts by the Pentagon, which already controls 90% of the roughly $40 billion the U.S. spends on intelligence annually, to take over more responsibility for gathering and analyzing intelligence. But Tenet's departure may set the stage for much larger changes. The 9/11 commission report, due out on July 26, is expected to call for the creation of a new Cabinet-level chief who would consolidate control over all the nation's disparate intelligence operations—an idea supported by Bush's rival for the White House, John Kerry, but opposed by both Tenet and Defense Secretary Donald Rumsfeld.

In intelligence circles the betting is that Bush will avoid tackling a contentious re-

ONE EXPERT'S VERDICT: THE CIA CAVED UNDER PRESSURE

By MICHAEL DUFFY WASHINGTON

The CIA that George Tenet leaves behind next month is a shadow of its imaginary self, a butt of jokes rather than the envy of the world. It is an agency that has become self-protective and bureaucratic; it is too reliant on gadgets rather than spies to steal secrets. Sometimes the CIA has simply been too blind to see what is hiding in plain sight. Tenet restored the agency's morale, but he leaves behind a string of spectacular intelligence failures.

And that may not be the worst of it. In his new book *A Pretext for War*, intelligence expert James Bamford alleges that the CIA not only failed to detect and deter the secret army of Muslim extremists gathering over the horizon in the late 1990s but also failed to take action when a group of Administration hard-liners, backed by the Pentagon chief and Vice President Dick Cheney, began to advance the case for war with Iraq in secret using data the CIA widely believed weren't supportable or were just plain false. Instead of fighting back, Bamford argues, the CIA for the most part rolled over and went along. The result was a war sold largely on a fiction, confected from unchecked rumor and biased informants.

A Pretext for War is probably the best one-volume companion to the harrowing events in the war on terrorism since 1996, chiefly because it focuses on the most difficult to pierce subject: the hidden machinery of U.S. intelligence. Bamford is a veteran chronicler of the spy world whose *The Puzzle Palace*, published in 1982, is still considered the classic account of the mysterious National Security Agency (NSA), which electronically snoops on friends and enemies overseas. His account of 9/11 and its aftermath is studded with new

details, including some about the undisclosed location known as Site R, an underground bunker on the Maryland-Pennsylvania border where the Vice President spent much of his time in 2001. Deep under Raven Rock Mountain, Site R "is a secret world of five buildings, each three stories tall, computer filled caverns and a subterranean water reservoir." It is just 11 km from Camp David.

Bamford maintains that before 9/11, the U.S.'s entire spook network was pretty much out to lunch. It was a community that had done its job well in the cold war

THE CHARGE: Tenet, standing on the left with Cheney,

and was looking for a reason to exist. By the late 1990s the NSA was becoming obsolete, unable to keep up with the pace of technological change. The NSA netted millions more conversations at its worldwide listening posts than it could translate or interpret. The agency spent billions to eavesdrop on chatter overseas that moved by satellite—only to see the world move to harder-to-steal digitized

FIGURE 22: *TIME's generally good quality reading environment is evident in the left column. However, the side bar, which stetched across the gutter to the facing page, is a different matter with the head in condensed caps and demi-bold sans body type set ragged right, all on dark grey. Illustrations were in color.*

My Big Cruising Boat That Sails Like a Finn

Barbara Ann is my fifth boat in the past 30 years. I almost never race, but I've always had high-performance boats. The performance bug bit me in the 1960s when I experienced the joy of planing in a Finn at Community Boating on the Charles River in Boston. Although I was never hefty enough to sail a Finn well, the simplicity of sail control with just a big, bendy, unstayed mast was my standard for the way a sailboat should work.

When we retired, we decided to move up from our Baltic 37 to something in the 50-foot range that we could live aboard. I wanted this boat to be a nimble performer that could be easily sailed singlehanded. We commissioned Sparkman & Stephens to design for us the ultimate 50-foot single-handed cruising machine. The company had just completed the plans for a 65-foot AeroRig sloop, and it suggested a similar design. It took nearly two years to launch *Barbara Ann*, a 52-foot AeroRig sloop, and while we were pleased with the boat's craftsmanship, we were less satisfied with the AeroRig's performance.

The boat was far more tender than we expected, suffered from excessive weather helm, tended to pitch a lot, and the sail controls had faulty hydraulics, nonexistent manual backups, and numerous other flaws. When we unstepped the mast, we discovered that it weighed 3,900 pounds, more than double its 1,800-pound design weight. Suddenly we knew why the boat was tender.

The spar builder, England's Carbospars, was at this point out of business, so we needed to replace the rig. The options available were disappointing. A retrofit with a conventional stayed rig had numerous problems with no real advantages. Mast position, deck reinforcement, and hull strength were all designed for an unstayed mast. I needed to find a freestanding-mast solution to save my dream from becoming a costly compromise.

I started to research freestanding carbon masts and contacted naval architect Eric Sponberg of St. Augustine, Florida (www.sponbergyachtdesign.com), who'd done the conversion to carbon on Freedom cat rigs. He mentioned that Composite Engineering's Ted Van Dusen had just completed a rig that sounded like what I was looking for. I contacted Ted, who sent me to visit Bruce Schwab in Newport the day before he was scheduled to leave on the Around Alone race in *Ocean Planet*.

As I learned more from Bruce about the *Ocean Planet* concept, I began to see parallels between the needs of this flat-out, spartan racer and my comfy floating home. We both sailed shorthanded, and we both were willing to break a few rules to achieve a

The unstayed *Barbara Ann*

nice-handling, fast boat. I contracted with Ted Van Dusen to make us a new rig. Ted designed the new sail plan and passed it by Robbie Doyle of Doyle Sailmakers for a reality check. Robbie suggested adding a 5-foot bowsprit to improve the balance of the rig and get rid of the weather helm. I wanted a self-tacking jib, and getting a track on the foredeck with a good sheeting angle was a problem. Bruce suggested a Hoyt Jib Boom, which we adopted.

Doyle made our new sails, the first made with the small-boat version of its Ocean Weave fabric, a strong and light material.

The result of all this engineering has exceeded my wildest expectations. Our new rig weighs in at 927 pounds, shaving a ton and a half from our weight aloft–and we went from tender to wonderfully stable. The mainsail could now be cut with maximum roach, and this, plus the larger jib, has added 27 percent to our sail area. Amazingly, we find we can carry this extra sail area easily because the rig tends to spill the gusts, and the very stiff custom battens tend to hold the shape of the main under all conditions. It's almost like having a solid wing, and the helm is neutral most of the time. The Hoyt boom has a similar effect on the jib. Our next addition is a 1,600-square-foot Doyle masthead utility power sail (UPS) for light-air reaching.

Because of the rich input we received throughout this project, everything fell together perfectly. The soft-luff jib furls easily on its Facnor SDG 12000 continuous-loop furler because of some amazing luff rope Bruce discovered at a Future Fibres shop (www.futurefibres.co.uk) in New Zealand. Bruce also supplied the latest running rigging from Samson ropes, including special Amsteel Blue and WarpSpeed lightweight, low-stretch rope for the halyards (see "Getting a Line on Cordage," July 2002, and "Getting the Most out of High-Tech Line," August 2002). The Dutchman mainsail-flaking system operates flawlessly, partially because of suggestions to oversize the Antal cars and customize the sail's battens. The list of little things that make this new rig sail so well goes on and on.

So I finally have my big cruising boat with the fun and performance of that Finn I sailed those many years ago. For more on *Barbara Ann*, visit her website (http://barbara-ann.net).

Bill Southworth

Bruce Schwab comments: To some degree, the excessive weight of Bill Southworth's original AeroRig was the consequence of a problem with the spar builder, not with the AeroRig concept. If the original mast had been built by a reputable AeroRig builder, it would've been close to the design weight of 1,800 pounds.

FIGURE 23: A neat layout — but for readability, it has four strikes against it. The body text is all bold, it is all sans serif, it is set left (ragged right) instead of justfiied, and it is printed in a strong blue. The blue ink appears 'softened' a little by printing over a light beige background, but the whole still makes for difficult reading. How many would read the article right through?

eye; it breaks up long articles. But the clear indication of the tests is that used too much, it also makes the text harder to read.

Readers commented that the bold text:

- Gave them the same feeling of fatigue experienced when text was printed in high or medium intensity colors.
- Occupied more of the letter space allocated to it than normal roman type, and so seemed to be cramped.
- Seemed to set up a halo effect, carrying the outline of letters into adjoining letters and on to the lines above and below.

Results

Table 4: Comprehension levels of text printed in bold versus text in roman. Good comprehension dropped by more than half; poor increased nearly fivefold. Averages of responses from all 224 subjects.

Comprehension levels	Good	Fair	Poor
Text in Times Roman	70	19	11
Text in Times Roman Bold	30	20	50

Is italic body type as black as it's painted?

Editors throughout the Latin script world have clung to the proposition, as though it were Holy Writ, that italic body type is illegible. There is, however, no reason why it should be true: italic letters do not offend by lack of any distinction that their roman counterparts have.

Serif italics (sans body types were not considered for this test) have the same thick and thin strokes, the same x-height of their vertical fellows, and, possibly a virtue, they slope in the direction of reading and of normal handwriting. What then, has brought italic body type into such disrepute? It is difficult to see. True, some italic faces have elaborate swashes on some letters and some are significantly condensed when compared with their roman counterparts — presumably in search of 'elegance' or a nearer alliance between italics and script.

Insofar as italics veer towards script faces, we would urge caution in their use but are 'ordinary italics' evil?

The procedure in this test was identical with that for the others; the body types used were Corona Light Roman and Corona Light Italic, 8 on 9 point. This is a face with minimal elaboration to and narrowing of the italics compared with the roman version.

Almost 20 years after the original *Rainbow Warrior* was bombed, the mark II ship continues its green global mission. Our journalist climbed aboard when the good ship came south.

"The day will come when the land is dry and the seas blacken, the fish flow dead in the rivers and the birds fall from the sky; that day people of all races and creeds will rise up like Rainbow Warriors, to return the Earth its beauty and harmony."

The words of 'Eyes of Fire', an elderly Cree Indian woman, spoken over 200 years ago.

Ship the *Rhein* is in Port Melbourne and, lit up against the night horizon, looks like a monstrous truck on the highway. Somewhere in the dark ocean, trailing behind, is Greenpeace's flagship the *Rainbow Warrior*.

The *RW*'s armada – complete with onboard campaigners dressed as GM chickens – is attempting to block the *Rhein*, a ship carrying 6300 tons of unlabelled genetically engineered soy. According to Greenpeace, GE soy is the largest source of GE contamination in Australian food. Much of the soy is used as poultry feed. In other words, we eat chickens raised on GE feed – and mostly we're unaware of the fact.

The original *RW* is now laid to rest near Nicholls' home in NZ, and is a tourist attraction (as well as an appropriate reef home for the sea creatures it defended). With a doubly thick hull, the new *RW* has avoided collisions for 15 years, according to Nicholls, who has been the skipper, on and off, for 10 of those years.

'Seriously committed crewmembers' make the ship what it is, according to Nicholls, and there are currently 15 crew (drawn from six nations). Over the years, some 3000 people from 100 countries have provided hands on deck.

What motivates crewmembers to put themselves on the line? I speak to Carlos, a deckhand from Spain. "I live in a developed country, it is good, and we have too much comfort," he says. "I hate sitting on the couch. On the *Warrior*, we prove that we can make a difference."

Andrew, an American with 14 stints on the *RW*, is the ship's communications officer. He is responsible for uploading media, gathering documentary evidence and maintaining the web diaries – all of which can make or break a campaign.

Indeed, Andrew believes the web diaries and online exchanges between crewmembers are particularly popular and inspirational.

THE RAINBOW CONNECTION

Thus the flotilla of protest boats here to make things difficult for the *Rhein*. Choppers buzz overhead. Police boats form an escort. The *RW*'s support craft – warned not to get within 50 metres of the *Rhein* – are tossed about by the ship's waves, like toy boats in a bath.

It's not until daylight that the *RW* herself appears. With her sails up – so the docked *Rhein* can't miss her – the *RW* cuts through the chilly diamond water into Port Melbourne.

The *RW* has been sorely missed – something I tell the captain when I receive permission to come aboard. "I keep her out of harm's way," replies Derek Nicholls, making an ironic reference to the fact he was arrested recently at a port south of Sydney for taking the *RW* where it wasn't permitted to be.

The ship is used to such rough adventure; through polar ice, typhoons and nuclear-bleached reefs, the *RW* has confronted (and exposed) oil spills, radioactive dumpings and illegal whaling on its travels.

"Rainbows give promise to fair-weather and calmer waters," says Nicholls, a 53-year-old New Zealander. "When people see the *Warrior*, they are reminded that things are brighter around the corner."

In 1985 the original *RW* was bombed in Auckland, New Zealand, as it was preparing for a major campaign against French nuclear testing. The ship's photographer, Fernando Pereira, was killed. Initially, the French government denied all knowledge of the terrorist act, but it soon emerged the bombing was the work of the French secret service, acting on orders.

Do the ship's opponents fear such open messages emanating from the *RW*'s satellite? "Dangerous people, like the armed timber mafia, don't fear anything – but they worry about information on illegal activities getting out," says Andrew.

A few years ago, the timber mafia – a name given to those involved in the $20billion-a-year organised crime of illegal logging – kidnapped *RW* crewmembers. Their unusual ransom? Influence over cyber-broadcasts.

The hostages eventually escaped, but kidnap and sabotage remain alongside crocodile and shark attacks as the major perils of working on the *RW*.

"It's a very close situation. We eat together and get arrested together," laughs Robin, the cook and one of three women on board. Robin cooks one solid meal a day for her 'floating family' (and despite what you might think, Robin says that "not everyone is vegetarian").

Life at sea is not all action and activism. The vast distances mean frequent stops; preparing to sail means long hours of training and technical planning. For these reasons, and others, the 'three months on, three months off' rule is mandatory.

But none of the crewmembers I spoke to were in any hurry to get off. They are off to another campaign, this time raising hell and bringing much needed attention to the world's depleted oceans.

As long as she sails, there will be many around the world watching this rainbow with interest and passion.

by Nicholas Montgomery *photograph courtesy of Greenpeace*

FIGURE 24: *A shocker! The type is reversed out of a blue sky and sea, shading to very light on one hand and near black on the other. The whole page is in sans serif, bold type. The headline cutting through the middle of the two columns of type does nothing to assist readers. The look will grab page flippers, but once stopped, will they read through the article?*

Results

Table 5: Comprehension levels of italic body type versus roman type.

Comprehension levels	Good	Fair	Poor
Corona Roman text	67	19	14
Corona Italic text	65	19	16

Conclusion

- Bolding may be fine for a few words or lines, but in some respects it resembles the application of color — bolded type makes too strong an impression on the reader's eye for sustained reading. Long text in bold was not well comprehended.
- Italic type, on the other hand, appears to be wrongly castigated — comprehension was not significantly affected. Readers indicated that while italic type caused an initial reaction because it was unusual in such volume, it caused no difficulty for them.

  It is not the intention to advocate widespread use of italic type as body matter — merely to challenge our typographical and design assumptions and find better ways of achieving our ends. In this case, it would appear that of the two most common methods of differentiating body matter from the general run of text, by bolding or using italics, the latter is better for comprehension.

FIGURE 25: Switching from roman to italic type makes little difference to reader comprehension; switching to bold loses half the audience.

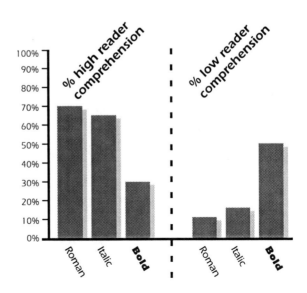

FIGURE 26: *Samples of roman and italic versions of fonts.*

Caslon with a small 'x' height is an elegant face in both roman and italics. Looking at it, you wonder where italic type acquired such an unsavory reputation.

Caslon with a small 'x' height is an elegant face in both roman and italics. The italics are just a little decorative and condensed and appear to be more readable at about one hundred and ten per cent width as shown here.

Times, a mainstay of the newspaper world, is like Corona, Century and a number of similar faces, simple and straightforward; best practice in tough printing conditions.

Times, a mainstay of the newspaper world, is like Corona, Century and a number of similar faces, simple and straightforward; best practice in tough printing conditions.

Galliard, on the other hand, while businesslike in roman (although just a little decorative) goes quite overboard in italics which are significantly narrowed and stylized. *No-one* should have to read a column of Galliard Italic!

Galliard, on the other hand, while businesslike in roman, goes quite overboard in italics. No-one *should have to read a column of Galliard Italic! Is this a giveaway to its origins — it was designed by Hermann Zapf, father of Zapf Chancery script?*

Helvetica is a mainstay of the sans serif face brigade; at once cursed for its plainness and praised for its clean, geometric shapes.

The sans variation on the italics theme is the oblique style, subjectively difficult enough to read in lower case BUT EVEN HEAVIER GOING IN CAPITALS.

FIGURE 27: The first of three pages, all in italics, to introduce the reader to Faye Kellerman's 'Prayers for the Dead'. Three pages of bold would be unthinkable in a book, yet designers happily condemn readers to page after page of bold in periodicals. Perhaps book designers can put readers first while magazine designers must sacrifice good reading for a dramatic 'look' to sell the product.

Prologue

'This is a team effort, Grace. You know that.'

Even through morphine-laden stupor, Grace knew that. From her hospital bed, she looked up at her doctor's face – a study in strength. Good, solid features. A well-boned forehead, Roman nose and a pronounced chin, midnight blue eyes that burned fire, tar-black hair streaked with silver. His expression, though grave, was completely self-assured. Someone who knew what he wanted and expected to get it. Truth be told, the man looked downright arrogant.

Which was exactly the kind of doctor Grace had wanted. What she hadn't wanted was some young stud like Ben Casey or an old fart like Marcus Welby with the crinkly eyes and the patient, understanding smile. She had wanted someone bursting with ego. Someone whose superiority was touted, worn with pride like Tiffany jewelry. A self possession that spoke: Of course the operation is going to be successful. Because I always succeed.

Because getting a new heart was serious business.

Grace Armstrong had to have the best and the brightest. Had the luxury to afford the best and the brightest. And in Dr. Azor Moses Sparks, she had gotten numero uno.

Dope was winning the battle of wits with Grace's brain. Sparks's face had lost clarity, sat behind a curtain of haze, his features becoming blurry except for the eyes. They peered through the muck like high-beam headlights. She wanted to go to sleep. But Sparks's presence told her she wasn't permitted to do that . . . not just yet.

He spoke in authoritative, stentorian tones. The sounds bounced around Grace's brain, words reverberating as if uttered through a

1

FIGURE 28: Centered lists are much loved by designers but are difficult for readers to use. Here the designer adds insult to injury by using condensed sans serif in upper case in a small size for the information blocks at the foot of the column.

FIGURES 29 (below left) & **30** (below right): Text made into design elements regardless of readability.

Left, Right, Centered, Justified?

FIGURE 31: *Ragged right, ragged left, centered and justified setting.*

Set left, ragged right setting was popularized by the designer, Eric Gill, in 1930 to eliminate the need in book setting for uneven letter and word spacings to fill out lines. It has some surface logic; we have all stumbled over horrendous spacing from time to time, particularly when text has been set too large in narrow columns.

But there's no such logic in ragged right's sinister offspring, set right/ragged left — and there often seems to be no overall design logic in its use either. It nearly always seems to be thrown in as if by chance. See figure 33 (p.58).

Centered type is ragged right *and* ragged left. Does it exhibit the worst characteristics of both? It was not tested in this series but its imaginary centre line may make it easier to comprehend than ragged left.

Fully justified type is often criticized for resulting in wide word and/or letter spacing as the layout program strives to make the best fit between the words and line length allowed. However, noticeable deviations from 'natural' spacing can be handled by sensitive use of the tools available.

There are those who argue that for legibility, all body type must be justified completely. Some accept type which is set ragged right, and some magazine and advertising designers who strive for effect rather than communication set body matter ragged left. Many type practitioners approve of ragged right setting yet steadfastly oppose ragged left. Those who accept ragged left setting usually accept ragged right too.

Centered text, while often serving well for headlines and short captions, is rarely seen in body matter although it sometimes appears — and interferes — in longish paragraphs which fall somewhere between a kicker head and an introductory paragraph, and in advertisements. Some designers

FIGURE 32: *Reduced to good and poor, the comprehension message is clear: justified type is best for readers with set left/ ragged right a poor second and set right/ragged left nowhere.*

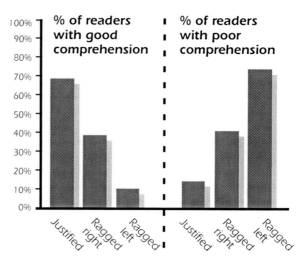

FIGURE 33: (below) Gravity is good. Why not put the head under the picture instead of reversing it out of the blue-black sky? Why the period? Good choice of body type, but why is it set right (ragged left) in a high actinic blue ink?

Since 1995, YachtWorld has been the premier channel for people to find their perfect boat by using the Internet to directly connect with more than 60,000 boats, represented by over 1,600 brokers worldwide. YachtWorld makes finding the boat of your dreams fast, easy and intuitive. Whether you are buying, selling or just starting to browse, with YachtWorld you save time and money. Once you locate boats that interest you, contact a broker advertising in Sailing World Magazine to learn more about your boats of interest and for guidance and professional assistance throughout the purchase process.

Visit www.yachtworld.com today and let us bring the boats to you.

WWW.YACHTWORLD.COM

appear to have a positive fetish for setting lists centered. They make very attractive shapes which are next to useless for actual reference.

To test this element of layout, readers were presented with papers with fully justified, ragged right and ragged left setting. It should be mentioned that setting had to be modified slightly to cater for the additional space required to accommodate ragged setting, and that the results apply to complete pages set ragged.

Type used was Corona Roman 8 point on 8½ point body, and the layout was identical to those used in tests on page design (figure 10, p.34).

Results

Table 6: Comprehension levels of text set justified, ragged right and ragged left. Percentages of all participants.

Comprehension level	Good	Fair	Poor
Fully justified	67	19	14
Ragged right	38	22	40
Ragged left	10	18	72

Conclusion

The conclusion must be that ragged setting should be avoided if comprehensibility is to be maintained.

- The comprehension level — or lack thereof — of ragged left setting was similar to that for sans serif body type, yet paradoxically many designers who would never use ragged left setting have no qualms about ordering considerable volumes of setting in sans serif type.
- It would be interesting if a future researcher were to quantify the comprehensibility of sans serif type set ragged left, as is seen frequently in some magazines and in display advertising. What effect does the double whammy have on readers' comprehension?
- The findings may not apply to small amounts of ragged setting, although subjectively, ragged left, particularly, will always seem more difficult because of the confusion over line starting and ending points as our eyes sweep over the text. See *How we read* (p.143).

FIGURE 34: Classic layout — picture, headline, body copy, contact. This picture is all red and gold, the 'distressed' type and background follow suit. Then they are tilted off horizontal. Nobody's going to read the script headline in a hurry (this gray scale version is easier to read than the original). Shown full size.

HEADLINE TYPE

David Ogilvy asserts that headlines are the most important part of an advertisement, because the headline can tell the reader whether he or she is a "prospect" for the topic. The same could be said with equal validity about editorial matter.

Therefore putting the right headline on an advertisement or article in the right words, the right shape, the right style, and in the right type, demands consideration. The right words are, patently, dependent on the context.

The style and shape are, to a degree, dependent on agency, newspaper or magazine house styles, or on design considerations. Within such constraints designers make choices about type, whether it be sans serif or serif, roman or italic, old face or modern, sans or gothic, script or decorative, capitals or lower case, set natural or kerned, stretched or condensed.

Serif versus sans serif — little to debate

There seems little to debate about the relative value of sans serif and serif type in headlines. In US research cited by Edmund Arnold, sans serif has been claimed as marginally more legible than serif, but the difference was too small to be considered statistically significant. The choice generally lies with whichever style best suits the publication or the tenor of the advertisement or article.

Capitals versus lower case

There is, however, much to debate about the relative value of capitals and lower case in headlines. From the early days of newspapers until the 1950s, capital letter headlines were almost an institution. Now, more than 75 per cent of newspapers in the western world use lower case headlines.

Editors who favor capitals claim they have more impact on readers; those who prefer lower case claim their preference gives greater legibility. The latter argument is easy to accept, compare the facility of reading this paragraph compared with the following one:

READING THIS PARAGRAPH IS A MUCH HARDER TASK. THE EYES HAVE TO GROPE FOR THE IDENTITY OF LETTERS, THENCE WORDS, TO COMPREHEND THE SENSE.

Yet, despite an apparent consensus in favor of lower case, a significant number of papers and magazines still make widespread use of capitals in heads, as a browse through almost any newsstand rack will quickly show.

Those who argue for lower case because of its apparently greater legibility have the physiology of reading on their side. Readers recognize letters primarily by the shape of their upper half. With lower case this is simple, because the top halves of lower case letters are generally distinctive, and importantly, framed by the white space that surrounds them, permitting easy recognition. This is illustrated in Figure 35 (opposite).

Put the headline in capitals, though, and the eye is presented with a solid rectangle, and recognizing the words becomes a task instead of a natural process.

Hybrid, script, cursive, ornamented faces

Unusual type faces for headlines come into vogue from time to time. The arguments in favor of their use generally follow those presented in support of all-caps — they are said to have impact and draw in readers.

Headline types with greater legibility

In the first test, answers were sought to two complex questions:
- Which headline faces and styles have greater legibility?
- Do capital letter headlines, "all caps heads" have greater impact than lower case headlines, and if so, is this sufficient to counterbalance any supposed loss of legibility?

The methods used in previous tests did not lend themselves to testing the legibility of headlines, and a different method was used.

The program's 224 readers were asked during the course of the study to look at a collection of headlines, set in a variety of type styles, and were asked: "Do you find this easy to read — yes or no?"

Headlines were all set in 36 point type, 27 picas (4½ inches, 11.5 centimeters) wide over two decks, and in medium or bold face, depending on availability. Care was taken that surrounding type elements did not distract from the headlines. In most instances, rectangles of stick-on screen, representing illustrations, and "greek" stick-on body type were used to support the headline.

The results reported in table 7 (p.65) and figures 37-39 (p.66) are expressed as percentages of the 224 readers who found the nominated

FIGURE 35: The top half of letters is more recognizable than the bottom, especially in lower case, making it easier to read.

Lower case

Look at the top half

Look at the top half

Look at the bottom half

Look at the bottom half

Look at the top half

Look at the top half

Look at the bottom half

Look at the bottom half

Upper case

Look at the top half

Look at the top

Look at the bottom half

Look at the bott

Look at the top half

Look at the top

Look at the bottom half

Look at the bottom

FIGURE 36: The sans serif bold for the headline and byline are fine, but a switch from justified serif body type to sans serif set left (ragged right) with very narrow column gutters makes reading the text no fun at all. It now takes longer to read and results in many readers losing much of the message.

Airport plan cops flak

By Todd Cardy

A PEAK retail body has accused Moorabbin Airport of switching its focus from aviation to shopping.

The Shopping Centre Council of Australia hit out in a submission on the airport's draft master plan, which maps the site's future for the next five years.

Feedback on the plan was handed to Federal Transport Minister John Anderson last Friday.

While the draft predicts less aircraft activity, it flags plans to expand commercial opportunities on the site to generate more money.

Shopping Centre Council executive director

Milton Cockburn blasted the airport's plan, saying it disadvantaged other shopping centre owners.

Mr Cockburn said he believed the airport's planning controls would be less strict than those imposed by local governments, which had the final say on other shopping centre developments.

"With the recent addition of traditional retailers to the (Aldi) supermarket development, Moorabbin Airport has become a supermarket based shopping centre," Mr Cockburn said.

Moorabbin Airport Resident's Association president Tom Uren was also unhappy, branding the airport corporation a "rogue planning authority".

Moorabbin Airport Corporation chief executive Phil McConnell refused to comment on the 13 submissions received in response to the draft.

In February, the corporation, which operates the airport under a lease from the Federal Government, released the Moorabbin Airport Preliminary Draft Master Plan for public comment.

The five-year review is a statutory requirement.

Mr Cockburn said although the draft plan would prohibit a department store-style development at the airport, current retailing could expand.

"This confirms our concerns that airport sites, with their privileged development control

processes, will gradually become de facto urban centres," he said.

Mr Uren said residents opposed any extension of the airport's runway, closure of the Moorabbin Public Golf Course or extension of the corporation's planning controls.

"What we are most concerned about is the total influx of traffic into the area if the airport is allowed to continue to expand its shopping," he said.

"Residents are worried that more commercial sites will ruin the area."

Mr Anderson has 90 days to comment on the draft plan before it is tabled in Federal Parliament.

headline type easy to read. Each reader was asked to pass judgment on several samples of each style. It is significant that each reader, having once declared a type easy or not easy to read, repeated that view when the same type, in a different context, was shown later in the program. Equal numbers of each style of heading were shown to the readers.

Results

The full results are given in Table 7 (opposite).

In summary, of the 24 types and styles shown, readers rated lower case old style and modern serif, sans serif and Optima, whether roman or italic/oblique, as a clear group at the top, the same faces in capitals plus square serif lower case in the middle group and square serif capitals, scripts, ornamentals and black letter faces at the bottom.

Capitals versus lower case

The difference in perceived legibility between lower case and capitals of the same type family was marked — the best lower case faces were in the 90 per cent bracket; the same faces in capitals rated down around 65 per cent, performing only two-thirds as well. See figure 37 (p.66).

Supplementary question: Impact of capitals

The justification for using capitals in headlines is often "impact". Is the perceived impact great enough to counter the apparent loss in legibility? About equal numbers claimed extra impact for both capitals and lower case. The results are summarized in figure 37 (p.66).

Regular faces or italic/oblique?

As in body text, there was little difference between regular and italic/oblique styles of the same type in lower case. Generally there were more differences between them in all capitals headlines. The results are given in Table 7 (opposite) and figure 37 (p.66).

The hybrid faces — Optima and Memphis

The 'humanist' face, Optima, has the thick and thin strokes of a serif face but no serifs, so it can be classified as sans serif, while conversely, the square serif face, Memphis, has the single thickness strokes of a typical sans serif type, but with serifs, so it can be classified as serif type.

Their contrasting performances are shown in table 7 (opposite) and figure 37 (p.66). Optima performed nearly, but not quite, as well as a regular sans serif type; Memphis performed well below both serif and

TABLE 7: Perceived legibility of headline type faces and styles — percentages of 224 readers who said the headline was easy to read.

Rank	Type and Style	%
1	Roman (serif) old style lower case	92
2	Sans serif lower case	90
3	Serif modern lower case	89
4	Serif old style italic lower case	86
5	Serif modern italic lower case	86
6	Sans serif oblique lower case	86
7	Optima lower case	85
8	Optima oblique lower case	80
9	Serif modern capitals	71
10	Serif old style capitals	69
11	Square serif lower case	64
12	Serif modern italic capitals	63
13	Serif old style italic capitals	62
14	Sans serif oblique capitals	59
15	Optima oblique capitals	57
16	Sans serif capitals	57
17	Optima capitals	56
18	Square serif capitals	44
19	Cursive or script lower case	37
20	Ornamented lower case*	24-32
21	Cursive or script capitals	26
22	Ornamented capitals*	11-19
23	Black letter lower case	10
24	Black letter capitals	3

* The ornamented faces came in various forms resulting in a range of responses.

FIGURE 37: *Regardless of the type face used, lower case headlines get a significantly higher legibility rating than do capitals in the same face.*

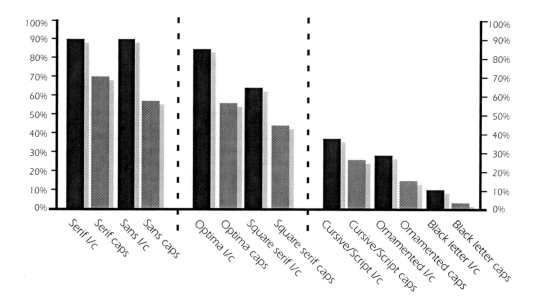

FIGURE 38: Serif italics and sans obliques (on left) versus cursive/script and ornamented faces. Even the worst of the conventional faces, Sans oblique capitals, rates between 50 percent and 400 percent better than the less conventional faces.

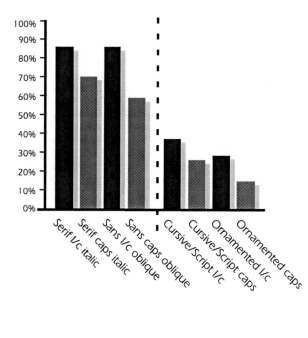

FIGURE 39: Which has greatest impact — all caps or lower case headlines? For most, there is no difference.

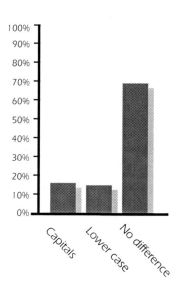

FIGURE 40: Fancy faces in headlines scored poorly and these two examples help illustrate why. The mystery word is Dubai (top). Enjoy your read (below).

sans types — so far below, in all caps, that it was in the "worst" group with the cursives, scripts and ornamented faces.

The usual serif types, which incorporate the thick and thin strokes of Optima and the serifs of square serif type, are the best performers of all. Given the arguments that rage around what makes a type face legible and attractive to read, there is room for some significant research here.

Script, cursive and ornamented faces

Designers of magazines, advertisements, brochures, annual reports and the street press seem to love headlines in unusual faces — usually citing their alleged impact compared with more conventional and more readable type. Since it has been demonstrated time and again, and surely is perfectly obvious anyway, that if a reader cannot readily read a headline, he or she will skip the body copy, any deviation from the best headline type must be open to question. The results of this series clearly shows that script, cursive and ornamented faces rate abysmally; at best, only a third as well as the best performers, serif and sans serif lower case. The comparative ratings are obvious in figure 37 (p.66). It might be thought the scripts and cursives would do better when compared with italic styles. They do not (figure 38, p.66).

Manipulated type

Unless otherwise specified, type samples used in this project were regular faces (not condensed), set 'natural', that is, spaced as the designer specified. The effect of kerning (reducing letter spacing or tight tracking) and condensing type were also considered.

Computers enable designers and typesetters today to do things with type that neither their predecessors, the hand and machine compositors, nor the typographers who designed the type, could have imagined. Type can be bent around corners or in circles for display advertising purposes; it can be squeezed or stretched horizontally or vertically, distorted in three dimensions ... the possibilities are virtually endless. But regrettably, this typographical cornucopia contains some questionable fruit. Kerning is one of these, condensing or stretching type is another.

Kerning/tracking

A kern in the days of hot metal or handset type was that part of a type letter which protruded above, below, or to the side of the body, for example, the curved finial of the letter 'f'. Now it is a computer process also called tracking, which gives the operator the ability to control interletter spacing precisely. With kerning, individual letters such as A and W can be closed up to the adjoining letter to obtain optically even letter spacing.

Kerning may be used because the headline writer wants another letter space or so to be able to fit in a message without going to a smaller font, but in most instances it appears to be purely for effect.

As more kerning units are employed the danger increases that letters become welded together. It must be asked whether kerning has an effect on type comprehensibility and at what stage does the effect begin.

To test this, two types, Times Roman and Helvetica, were chosen from those families which registered highest in the headline legibility test. They were set in 36 point capitals and lowercase, bold, set naturally, and kerned one, two, three and four units, as in figure 41 (p.70).

The procedure was identical to the previous headline legibility test.

Results

The test showed that one unit kerning had little effect on legibility. It decreased legibility in serif type, and increased it in sans serif, but minimally on each occasion. Kerning two and three units had a much more pronounced effect. Kerning four units had readers in dire trouble.

Table 8: Perceived legibility — percentages of 224 readers who said the headline was easy to read.

Type & Kerning	Lower case	Capitals
Times Roman		
Natural	93	68
Kerned one unit	92	66
Kerned two units	67	53
Kerned three units	44	41
Kerned four units	0	0
Helvetica Bold		
Natural	92	55
Kerned one unit	93	56
Kerned two units	79	48
Kerned three units	74	44
Kerned four units	0	0

FIGURE 41: Kerning/tracking — altering interletter spacing. From top — very loose, loose, natural/normal (as designed), tight, very tight.

Communicating or making shapes
Communicating or making shapes
Communicating or making shapes
Communicating or making shapes
Communicating or making shapes

When letters merge ...

Compounding the problem of tightly kerned or tracked headlines is that, with multiple deck (line) headlines, often the *interlinear* space is also kerned, and the ascending letters on lower lines commit acts of gross indecency on descending letters in the line above. Even worse is the all caps horror when both letters and lines merge to make a solid block. The effect of this was shown in the title of the first publication produced from these studies and distributed by the Australian Newspaper Advertising Bureau (figure 42, opposite).

It is when letters merge, as in the secondary headline, that the reader cries: "Hold! Enough!"

Not one reader in the study indicated that headlines in which the letters merged were easy to read. The comprehension level was a flat zero.

Notes

Traditional type units are discussed in Appendix 4, *Typographical Terms*. The layout or graphics programs available today might not use the one, two, three or four units mentioned here. The eyes should be the guide.

When kerning, it is important to consider the medium on which the work is to be printed. A headline kerned three units may look fine on a laser print, but if printed on newsprint, ink absorption could cause the letters to bleed into one another. A classic example of this appeared in the newspaper headline: 'Jogging burns excess energy'. The letters 'r' and 'n' in the word 'burns' bled together. The result is obvious! Notice how the same level of kerning works fine with the first three letters of 'excess'.

Jogging burns excess energy

FIGURE 42: The original title of the monograph in which these research results were published. In the study, no readers reported preferring merged letters.

Communicating
OR JUST MAKING
PRETTY SHAPES

Squeeze or stretch

Another questionable area is stretching or squeezing type into extreme extended, condensed or distorted styles. Back in hot metal days, type came in four basic widths — expanded, natural, condensed and extra condensed. With digitized typesetting on the desktop, type can be distorted in all sorts of ways to suit the designer's or typesetter's imagination — or, possibly to try the reader's patience — and all pretty much at the click of a mouse.

But should technology serve only the designer and headline writer, or should it also serve the reader? Are we, by distorting type, discomfiting the reader to such an extent that he or she will retaliate by the only means open to them — refusing to read our message?

If this danger is real, how far down the primrose path can we go before our use of the technology available to us becomes counter-productive?

To find answers to some of these questions, a further research program with a sample of 500 was conducted in Sydney in the winter of 1986. It looked at one of the simplest distortions — condensing type.

Results

The findings were:

- The point at which headlines, when condensed, become difficult to read appears to be at 70 per cent of natural width (in fact, the width of most type foundry condensed faces). Nearly 40 per cent of the sample indicated this point and a further 44 per cent indicated the threshold at three per cent above or below this width in all styles shown to participants.

- The point of condensing at which headlines were deemed easiest to read was at 90 per cent of natural setting. About 40 percent of the sample indicated this, with a similar percentage nominating a width three percent above or below the 90 per cent width.
- The style of headline setting deemed easiest to read was lower case condensed to 90 per cent of natural width, with no difference noted between sans serif and serif headlines. Where a choice of type was offered, all participants deemed lower case easier to read than capitals.

Conclusions on headlines

- The most legible headlines are those in lower case.
- There is little to choose between old style and modern serif types and sans serif (including 'humanist' typefaces) in headlines, or between roman/regular and italic/oblique styles.
- All capitals headlines lose significantly in legibility.
- There is little or no perceived extra impact of headlines in all capitals.
- Square serif capitals, scripts, particularly decorative ones, ornamental faces and black letter faces are the least legible in headlines.
- Reducing letter spacing, negative/minus kerning or tracking, should be kept to a minimum to avoid loss of legibility.
- Merging letters into each other through reductions in interletter and interlinear spacing kills legibility. It might make pretty shapes, but it does not communicate.
- A reduction of letter width to 90 per cent is fine in either serif or sans serif type, lower case, produces the "most readable" headline according to participants in this study. Reducing the width of letters beyond that is questionable for readers as is increasing the width of letters.

FIGURE 43: Type stretched, natural and condensed. Readers prefer headlines in lower case and condensed to 90 per cent width.

Stretched to 150% width

Natural (as designed)

Condensed to 90% of natural

Condensed to 70% of natural

Condensed to 50% of natural

FIGURE 44: Some fairly extreme manipulation which makes type virtually unreadable — and is not uncommon in both editorial and advertisements. Such manipulation was not tested in this series of studies.

DID YOU EVER TAKE A VACATION THAT
MADE YOU FORGET YOU HAD A JOB BACK HOME?

THAT MADE YOU FORGET THERE WAS A "BACK HOME"?

Indulge in a truly intimate getaway when you sail with Tradewinds. Our personal vacation guides will take care of everything, from luggage to chart briefings to supplies, allowing you more time to relax and enjoy your vacation. For more information on bareboat or crewed charters from Tradewinds, call or visit our website.

800.825.7245   804.594.0881   www.tradewindyachts.com

TradeWinds
LUXURY CHARTER YACHTS

We take your vacation personally.

TORTOLA   ·   ST MARTIN   ·   ANNAPOLIS   ·   FLORIDA KEYS

BLACK VERSUS COLOR

Black is beautiful

Henry Ford was talking about mass production and cutting the costs of making cars when he famously said: "They can have any color so long as it's black!" But his dictum applies as well or better to questions of type and layout, with the possible extension to: "black and white".

The use of colored text in both headlines and body type, and text printed on colored tints, has proliferated with the rapid growth of the availability of cheap multiple color printing — from home output through inkjet printers and color laser printers through limited runs on digital printing presses to multimillion runs on high speed, multicolor presses. It is also ubiquitous on websites and in projected presentations.

Consider the page you are looking at now. It looks very much like any other page, with its ordinary black type printed on ordinary white paper. Now imagine coloring the type blue — how much more attractive the page might become to the reader's eye!

If you were to show potential readers the two pages together, the chances are that eight out of ten would find the blue printed page more attractive than the one with type printed black, and that nine out of ten would probably describe the black printed page as boring.

But ask those people now to read the two pages, and we are in a different ball game.

The chances are that around seven out of ten who read the black text would display comprehension sound enough to answer specific questions on the text and act on any message it contains, but that result would be turned on its head among those who attempted to read the visually more attractive page printed in colored text.

And that's not a very attractive result, you will agree, particularly if a lot of money has been invested in the text to sell a product!

FIGURE 45 (left): Great appearance in tones of orange-brown (PMS 173?). But does the visual art effect overcome the reading negatives introduced? Light sans serif body type printed orange-brown over light grey shapes makes for tough reading. Other negatives: curved lines and all caps head in 'distressed' type.

Spot color in print

Spot color — a second color, additional to the standard black, introduced into a page — can do wonders for the advertising revenue of publications and for response to advertisements and advertisers' sales. This is unassailable. US research tells us about an advertiser who paid a loading of 70 per cent for spot color and drew nearly 400 per cent more sales. Spot color generally adds to the cost of an advertisement by 20 per cent or more, but the advertisement is noted by 63 per cent more people and results in 64 per cent more sales.

What the research doesn't tell us is how the color was used. One can understand a positive impact when spot color is used for logotypes and ideograms such as BP, Shell, Ford, the Mitsubishi diamonds, 'Coke' and so on, but what about headlines? Or the text?

What's the effect on the reader if the color is used as part or all of the message, instead of as an ancillary?

Color in headline type

There is no doubt that color imparts a feeling of excitement and is a magnet for the eyes. The question we asked in these tests is:

- Does using color in headlines mean we get our message through to more readers/customers?

  This translates into three questions:

- Does color used in headlines or text impede comprehension of the total message — can that magnet impart a negative influence?
- Do high and low chroma color have the same effects?
- What is the position on balance, taking into account the acknowledged positive influence of the colored text acting as an eye magnet to attract more readers/customers and the influence (positive, neutral or negative) on comprehension of the messages conveyed in the body text.

Tests were made of both high chroma and low chroma colors. The stock used for this series of tests was, as with all tests, non-reflective.

High chroma color headlines

Most frequent use of color in headlines is high chroma color, such as the process colors, cyan and magenta. Other high chroma colors, such as hot red, bright green and orange are common in newspapers and magazines as run of press color availability has become virtually universal.

In the first tests, colors used were magenta (process red), cyan (process blue), hot red (100 parts magenta, 100 yellow), hot orange (100 yellow, 40 magenta), and lime green (100 yellow, 40 cyan).

The test procedure was identical to previous ones, with the obvious exception that color headlines were substituted for black headlines.

Results applying to each individual color were so similar as to enable a general conclusion to be drawn about high chroma color headlines — they attract the eyes but seriously interfere with comprehension of body text which follows. There was considerable comment from readers:

- Sixty-one per cent of all readers said they found high chroma colors most attractive, drawing their attention quickly to the text.
- Forty-seven per cent said they then found the headings hard to read.
- Sixty-four per cent said they found the color intruding while they were trying to read the text.
- Twelve per cent said they felt the same effect as an obtrusive light, or an over-bright color television picture, distracting the eyes.
- Ten per cent found the high chroma colors intense and tending to cause eye-tiredness.

Low chroma color headlines

The tests for low chroma colors were done in an identical manner.

The low chroma colors chosen were deep blue (100 parts cyan, 50 black), dark emerald (100 yellow, 100 cyan, 40 black); purple (100 cyan, 100 magenta); and plum red (100 magenta, 60 black). Comments made on these tests implied that these low chroma colored headlines did not have the same magnetic quality that the high chroma colors had.

However, there was a degree of attraction, in both positive and negative aspects. The good comprehension levels in this test were three times as high as those where high chroma colored headlines were used — but still down by 15 percentage points on the results for black headings.

Results — headline color

Table 9: Comprehension levels of black body text under colored headlines as percentages of all 224 readers.

Comprehension level	Good	Fair	Poor
With black headlines	67	19	14
High chroma headlines	17	18	65
Low chroma headlines	52	28	20

FIGURE 46:

Comprehension of text under headlines of different colors. Looking at the best and worst outcomes graphically highlights the dramatic loss of comprehension of text under a high chroma headline.

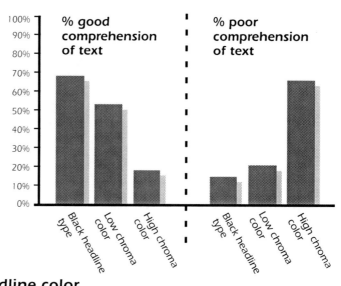

Conclusion — headline color

Comments made by readers and the comprehension test results both show that the use of process colors in *headlines* endangers readability and comprehension of the *message which follows in the text.* The high chroma spot color headlines antagonized some readers so much that two per cent of them indicated afterwards that, anxious to continue the test to the best of their ability, they folded the pages over to mask the colored headlines so they could concentrate better on reading the text. Inspection of retrieved papers confirmed this had occurred.

Their action was a dramatic demonstration of just how intrusive high chroma color type is. They could not simply choose to ignore it; they had to remove it from sight! This extreme reaction should act as a grim warning to high chroma colorphiliacs amongst designers!

The study shows that the darker the headline, the greater the comprehension level of the message under it. This poses the question: why not black? Ink doesn't come any darker! Should we place a 'black' ban on spot color in headlines?

Obviously, there is a paradox here. To be valuable as an eye catching device, a colored headline needs to be in a vibrant color, but that same color tends to disqualify it as a means of communication!

Used judiciously and sparingly, color can be a most compelling and useful feature, but clearly great care should be taken that the color doesn't get in the way of the message. Perhaps the real solution to mixing color and headlines is to keep the type black (or very dark) as far as possible — and use color in non-type forms.

Colored body type

So what happens when the body text is printed or rendered in color — again, something that is becoming increasingly popular in publications ranging from community newsletters to the glossiest of magazines — and almost universal on the internet?

To answer a range of questions in relation to this, tests were run using body text printed in:

- Black and several colors on white paper.
- Black and several colors on tinted paper.
- Black on shades of grey.
- Reverse, using black and color.
- Bold type, contrasted with the normal medium density type used in advertising and newspaper editorial for body text.
- Text printed on matt paper versus glossy paper. Note: differences in the first series on this dimension were not statistically significant so this variable was abandoned.

For the color text studies, articles presented to the readers were set in 10 point Times Roman type over 12 picas (two inches/five centimeters) to a depth of 18 centimeters (seven inches), three columns to a page. Each article had a single line heading set in 36 point Univers bold lower case printed black, placed above the three legs of text.

The layout and type employed were in a format which previous research had shown offers minimal distraction for the reader, thus enabling the text matter in its varied hues to stand or fall on the merits of those hues.

Articles were presented to 224 readers in six colors: black; PMS 239, deep purple; PMS 286, French blue; PMS 399, olive green, the muted color; and in two high chroma colors, warm red and process blue (cyan), all printed on white paper.

Results — body type color

When the text was printed black, the comprehension levels were similar to those obtained in previous tests conducted on similarly designed materials. The responses to text printed in colors showed a considerably lower level of good comprehension.

Some of the results were a surprise; comments by readers suggest there is more than one problem associated with reading colored text. One they identified was brightness, another was lack of contrast which occurred with both bright and muted colors. The results and comments suggest that text printed in color is a massive can of worms!

The results of the comprehension tests are shown in full in table 10 and dramatized in figure 47 (opposite). They are expressed as percentages of all 224 readers who participated in this series.

At the conclusion of each test on colored text, participants were asked to comment on the presentation of each paper. A summary of comments, collected for anecdotal purposes, is:

- Seventy-six per cent said they found text printed in high intensity colors difficult to read. The color tended to break concentration and many found they lost their place and had to recapitulate. The brightness of the color appeared to cause lines to merge, making reading difficult. There was no variation in the extent of this effect between text set in process blue and warm red.

- An analysis of questions and answers showed that few readers retained any comprehension of the text printed in bright colors beyond the first few paragraphs.

- Forty-one per cent of readers indicated there was insufficient contrast between brightly colored text and the paper background, despite the intensity of the color.

- Sixty-eight per cent indicated the same effect when the text was printed in olive green (PMS 399).

- On being shown pages printed in black and in cyan, 90 percent said they found the black page boring when compared with the blue printed page.

- Eighty-one per cent said they would prefer to read the page of colored type because it was more attractive. *But the test results clearly show that in practise, they found colored text more difficult to read. It was attractive to look at but did not make a good reading environment.*

- Sixty-three per cent said the medium intensity color, PMS 286, provided concentration problems. Again, lines of type appeared to merge. This phenomenon occurred less with the low intensity color (deep purple) and hardly at all with black.

- All the readers who exhibited poor comprehension of the text printed deep purple (36 per cent of the sample) said they believed their concentration suffered simply because they were aware the text was not printed black.

- Every reader said he or she preferred to read text printed in black.

TABLE 10: Comprehension level demonstrated by readers of text printed in different colors, as percentages of all 224 readers.

Comprehension level	Good	Fair	Poor
Text printed in black	70	19	11
Low intensity color (PMS 259)	51	13	36
Medium intensity color (PMS 286)	29	22	49
Muted color (PMS 399)	10	13	77
High intensity color (cyan/red)	10	9	81

FIGURE 47: Charting "good" vs "low" emphasizes the dramatic loss of reader comprehension when body text is printed in color instead of black on white paper. Who would want to shovel around 85 percent of all readers into the "low comprehension" bin, meaning they read and/or understand little of an advertisement or article? Yet this is what happens when type is printed in popular muted and high intensity colors.

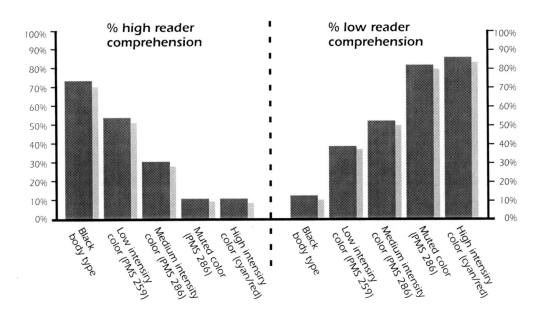

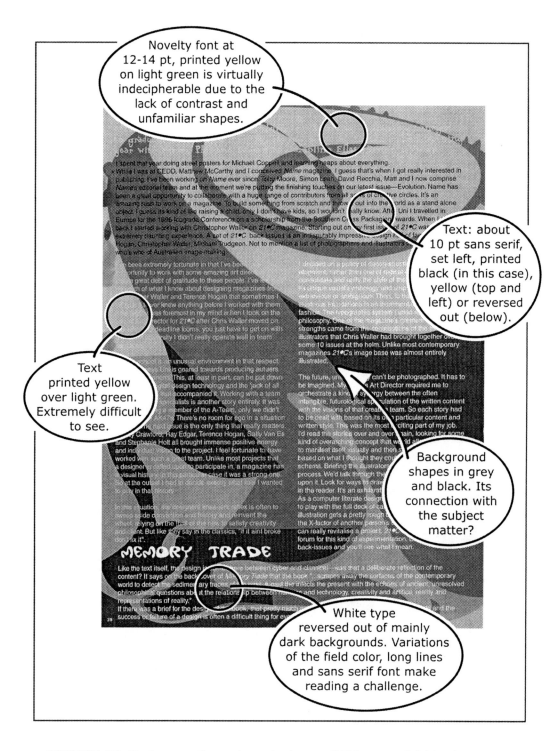

FIGURE 48: *Designer unfettered; reader ignored! This was a full bleed magazine page.*

Color on color

The use of colored text in both headlines and body type printed on same color tints has fallen in and out of fashion over the years, but has surged in popularity along with the development of what is now the near universal availability of cheap color output both in print and projected forms. The internet is awash with color on color.

Miles Tinker, in his *Legibility of Print* (Iowa State University Press, 1963), held that there should be at least 70 per cent differential between text and background — that is, if the text is printed solid (100 per cent ink), then the background should be no more than 30 per cent tint.

Obviously, this might be held to apply for black, or dark colors such as deep purple, navy blue or dark brown. But what about cyan, or magenta, which are much lighter to start with? What effect does printing text in cyan on a 30 per cent cyan tint have on the reader?

A second series of tests was conducted, using identical methodology, into the comprehensibility of text printed on tinted backgrounds.

Seven separate series of tests were conducted, using black on cyan

FIGURE 49: Text printed 100 per cent black on 30 per cent black screen (top) and the gray-scale equivalent of 100 per cent cyan on 30 per cent cyan screen (bottom).

This text is printed in black on 30% tint of black. Miles Tinker says this 70% differential retains sufficient contrast to ensure legibility. Not everyone agrees.

This text is equivalent to cyan on a 30% tint of cyan. Miles Tinker says this 70% differential retains sufficient contrast to ensure legibility. Not everyone agrees.

FIGURE 50: Darker screens seriously reduce contrast between type and field.

Text printed on a 10% screen.

Text printed on a 20% screen.

Text printed on a 30% screen.

Text printed on a 40% screen.

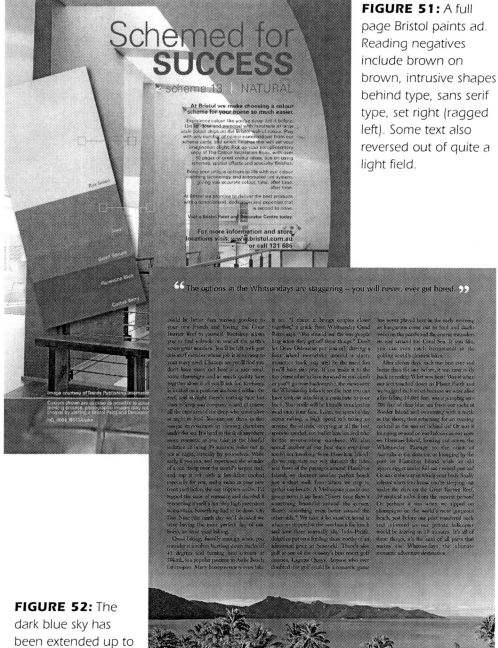

FIGURE 51: A full page Bristol paints ad. Reading negatives include brown on brown, intrusive shapes behind type, sans serif type, set right (ragged left). Some text also reversed out of quite a light field.

FIGURE 52: The dark blue sky has been extended up to be a background for the whole page. The black type disappears into it, especially the thinner parts of this serif type.

tints; PMS 259, deep purple, on its tints; PMS 286, French blue, on its tints; cyan, on its tints; black on tints of PMS 399, olive green; and PMS 399, olive green, on its tints; and black on screens of black.

Readers were given samples with text printed on tints of 10 percent of the base color, and increased in strength in increments of 10 per cent. Again, readers were invited to comment on the presentation of the text.

- More than half of those who responded made a comment with an interesting marketing application: at low strength, the tint seemed to soften the 'harshness' of the white paper, making it easier to read (this supposed harshness had not been mentioned before, nor was it mentioned afterwards). *But the test results did not show any increase in comprehension.*

- At high strength, the tint intruded and made reading more difficult. *The test results confirmed this effect.*

- Participants reacted more strongly to these tests than to any other aspect of the program.
  - In the test of cyan on a 10 per cent tint of cyan, 42 per cent of readers indicated they had not attempted to continue reading seriously after a few paragraphs.
  - When the tint was increased to 20 per cent, the percentage of "conscientious objectors" rose to 53 per cent.
  - This declared stance was supported by an analysis of the results. For example, in the tests with cyan on a 20 per cent cyan tint, 99 per cent of correct answers related to questions in the first leg of text, indicating a reluctance or inability to digest the entire article. Readers blamed the apparent brightness of the color and their difficulty in distinguishing text from background for their reading difficulty. The brightness element applied also during tests using PMS 286, French blue. The same articles were quite well comprehended when presented in black on 20 per cent cyan.

- Similar results were apparent in the test of PMS 399, olive green, on tints of the same color, except that brightness wasn't a problem. The principal reason given was the similarity in color of text and ground.

- Readers said they found the test using PMS 259, deep purple, on its 10 percent tint, pleasant to the eyes, but many said they were conscious of the presence of the color, which may have affected concentration.

- A frequent comment in the black on black screen test was that when the screen reached 20 per cent and higher, the words were more difficult to discern. It was like trying to "read a newspaper in poor light".

Results — body type, color on color

As in other tests, the comprehension level figures represent percentages of all 224 participants. *Tests were discontinued when it was judged that further testing would not add meaningful information, defined as when the combined results for good and fair totalled less than fifty per cent.*

Table 11: Black type on cyan tints.

Comprehension level	Good	Fair	Poor
10% tint	68	24	8
20% tint	56	21	23
30% tint	38	19	43
40% tint	22	12	66

Table 12: Cyan type on cyan tints.

Comprehension level	Good	Fair	Poor
10% tint	6	7	87
20% tint	0	2	98

Table 13: PMS 259, deep purple, type on its tints.

Comprehension level	Good	Fair	Poor
10% tint	50	14	36
20% tint	32	10	58

Table 14: PMS 286, French blue, type on its tints.

Comprehension level	Good	Fair	Poor
10% tint	27	16	57
20% tint	12	10	78

Table 15: Black type on PMS 399, olive green, tints.

Comprehension level	Good	Fair	Poor
10% tint	68	26	6
20% tint	53	21	26
30% tint	32	19	49
40% tint	22	13	65

Table 16: PMS 399, olive green, on its tints.

Comprehension level	Good	Fair	Poor
10% tint	8	8	84
20% tint	2	6	92

Table 17: Black type on black screens.

Comprehension level	Good	Fair	Poor
10% tint	63	22	15
20% tint	33	18	49
30% tint	3	10	87

FIGURE 53: Tables 10-17 summarized. Black printed on a 10 per cent screen of itself or a color is comprehended at close to black on white levels. Comprehension rapidly falls off as the density of the screen increases. In general, a color printed on a screen of itself is a serious problem for readers.

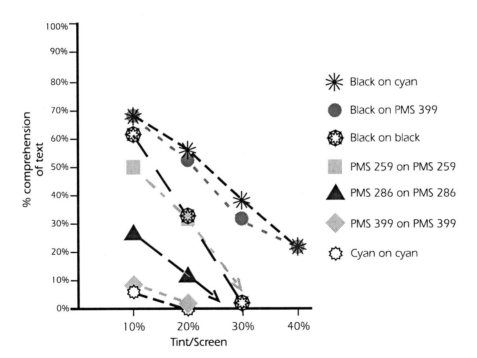

Supplementary question — Color on color as eye magnet

Prior to the tests, readers were shown, simultaneously, printed pages in all three forms (black on white, black on tint, and color on tint) and asked to make subjective judgments on their relative attractiveness.

It is interesting to compare the results of this test with the earlier experiment into the attractiveness of black and colored text on white (see page 80) *in which 90% of subjects said they found colored type more attractive.*

Table 18: Readers' assessments of attractiveness of print on a colored screen, expressed as percentages of all readers.

Print & Field color	"Most attractive"
Cyan	
Black text on white paper	8
Black text on 10% cyan	88
Cyan text on 10% cyan	4
PMS 399, olive green	
Black text on white paper	17
Black text on 10% PMS 399	83
PMS 399 on 10% PMS 399	0

Conclusion

Overall, these results provide several important messages to those designing and producing printed matter for any purpose:

- Black text printed on a light tint is an attractive marketing proposition, acting as an eye magnet in addition to having high comprehensibility. The extra cost of second color may well be more than justified, and designers can use light screens of color to lift or emphasize black type elements with confidence that they will not interfere with the reader's comprehension of the text content.
- Colored type on same tints should be avoid, except when the color is of low intensity and dark and the tint is light — 10 per cent and certainly not more than 20 per cent. Brighter colors on same color tints seriously interfere with reader comprehension *and repulse readers rather than attracting their interest.*

Peace be with us

● In the US recently, I attended a couple of deeply inspiring interfaith services that, for me, were unexpectedly ruffled by a request from one individual for prayers for American service people currently serving in Iraq. I am aware that the US is not only the most powerful nation on earth but also among the most unselfconsciously patriotic. Even so, in an interfaith setting, the request was troubling.

Years ago Professor Hans Kung, a leading Catholic theologian, predicted that there could be no peace on earth until there is peace between religions. The growing interest in interfaith as a tiny ballast to religious isolationism and divisiveness is an acknowledgment of this. Interfaith doesn't demand a dilution of anyone's individual religious beliefs. It does, however, practically

on the shores of the Hudson River opposite West Point, one of the world's richest military institutions. Looking out towards West Point's lavish buildings, it was impossible not to wonder what kind of world we would live in if we dared to fund "peace-readiness" on anything like the scale that we fund "war-readiness"; or if our most prestigious public institutions were those that researched and promoted peace; or if our "best and bravest" dreamed of getting into peace studies courses because we, as a society, valued peacemaking above all else.

On this anniversary of the September 11 terrorist attacks, it seems timely to remind ourselves that peacemaking is a complex and demanding human activity. It is far more complex and demanding than using force and state-sanctioned

We can't work effectively for peace while the "final solution" of war remains an option.

demonstrate that people from different faiths can come together in mutual "good faith" to support and learn from one another. They may – or may not – learn something about God in the process. They will certainly learn something about the universality of humankind's longing for God. The "patriotism" of their individual faith backgrounds does not preclude this.

At the second of those services, in one of New York's largest cathedrals, we received sacred teachings, readings and music from most faith traditions. This rich feast was a fearless celebration of diversity. So the request to pray for American service people came as quite a shock.

Clearly, I found it irritating that American patriotism was refusing to lie down. But I was more seriously troubled by the fact that even in this interfaith context, with its explicit commitment to healing divisions, there was an acceptance by at least one person taking part in the service that going to war might be a reasonable "solution" to human problems. And that the service people fighting that war, or any other, might be more deserving of prayer and concern than, say, those out there "fighting" to bring relief to the victims of war, injustice or poverty.

Oddly enough, just days earlier I had come back from an interfaith retreat in a former Catholic monastery that sits

violence to "solve" human problems. It is so demanding, in fact, that we can barely imagine it. Yet without imagining it, we will never achieve it.

Peacemaking is not about ending all conflict or even the likelihood of it. We are constantly in conflict even within our own minds; conflict will always exist outside ourselves also. The crucial challenge is learning ways to deal with conflict intelligently while constantly examining everything that contributes to it.

In the US, and in Australia, there are currently institutes for peace. That they are small and poorly funded is not just because war so significantly fires up the global economy, it's also because to the general public, in Australia as well as in the US, the idea of war – even the ideals of war – remains acceptable.

Peacemaking requires a profound and uncomfortable reworking of our old allegiances. We can't work effectively for peace while the "final solution" of war remains an option. Those two ideas are not compatible. Nor can we talk with any degree of honesty about "one humanity" or the potential benefits of interfaith study and dialogue while also assuming it's okay to kill the people with whom our government currently disagrees. The facts are stark. But I fear millions more lives will be lost before we see them. ■

www.stephaniedowrick.com.au

FIGURE 54: Columns of sans serif type set ragged right and printed black on a dull brown do not make for easy reading. The pull out printed in black and red and cutting across both legs of text, is a hurdle for readers.

FIGURE 55: A full magazine page ad. The surround is medium brown, with Avant Garde light reversed or printed darker brown on it. Long lines of tiny text at the foot are store contacts. Designed to be read or just looked at?

FIGURE 56: *Porsche fanciers read tough. Not only is the body type reversed out of glossy black, but the pull out is bright red, grabbing attention. A very rugged reading environment.*

FIGURE 57: *A summary box, a variation on a list, where readers should go for quick and easy access to basic information. Quick? Easy? The reading negatives include the information bites presented as continuous lines across the width of the magazine page, the small sans serif type and long lines, and the type being reversed out of a lightish blue. How many prospects just don't bother?*

Reversed body text

Designers often claim that reversed out type, that is, type which appears white or paper color in a black or colored field, grabs readers' attention and forces them to read the text. We are not talking about a short headline here, but whole blocks or pages of body matter. Some qualify the claim by specifying that the reversed out body type must be sans serif since the fine lines of serif type may be lost.

To test these two claims, articles were set reversed in 10 point serif and sans serif type printed on white paper.

Results

When the type was reversed, comprehension levels plummeted compared with the baselines: the same faces printed black on white (which produced results comparable to those of the earlier serif versus sans serif tests).

Table 19: Comprehension of matter printed in reverse using serif or sans serif type and a variety of background colors. Figures are percentages of 224 readers.

Comprehension level	Good	Fair	Poor
Serif type			
Text printed black on white	70	19	11
White on black	0	12	88
White on PMS 259, deep purple	2	16	82
White on PMS 286, French blue	0	4	96
Sans serif type			
Text printed black on white	14	25	61
White on black	4	13	83

Participants commented that there appeared to be a "light vibration", similar to, but worse than, that encountered when text was printed in high intensity colors, which made the lines of type seem to move and merge into one another. *Eighty per cent reported this phenomenon.*

Conclusion

- A reversed out page might look dramatic, but clearly, it is the enemy of reader comprehension.
- Sans serif type *is* better than serif type in reverse — but only if you are

FIGURE 58: The test results make it quite clear; reversed out text in any face on any color is just plain awful for readers.

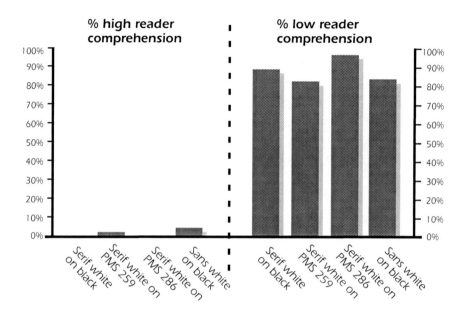

FIGURE 59: All caps printed dull blue on two tones of dull blue with shapes added might make an interesting design but are a challenge for readers even when the message amounts to only a few lines. Should the kicker end with a full point?

happy to accept "better" as being just four per cent good comprehension which, of course, is a ridiculous proposition if you really are in the business of communicating!

- Note that we are talking about a significant block of body text here, not just the word or two often seen as the reversed out head over a small article.

Matt versus glossy paper

Initially tests were conducted separately on matt and gloss paper. However, results showed little variation in good comprehension levels and it was noted that when readers experienced discomfort because of reflection from the glossy surface, they simply altered their position or the position of the paper, to minimize the problem. With no significant differences showing up, glossy as a variable was abandoned.

Conclusion overall

David Ogilvy said that advertising copy should never be set in reverse, nor over grey or colored tint. The old school, he said, "believed these devices forced people to read the copy; we now know that they make reading physically impossible".

- The results of tests on text printed in black on light color tints contradict his view — in fact, they support the "old school" in showing that they are eye magnets while retaining good reader comprehension.
- The tests on black text set on shades of grey or dark color text set on same color tints are more on his side.
- The tests on high chroma colored text printed on tints of itself support Ogilvy, showing such a combination does *not* attract readers and is the enemy of comprehension.
- The test text printed in reverse on black or dark colors supports his view to the hilt.

It is impossible to avoid the fact that comprehensibility of colored text increases as the color gets closer to black. So why not use black and employ color where it's best suited, as a complement to the message?

We should consider carefully Edmund Arnold's advice: "Start with good typography — the kind that best suits the reader — and use color to reinforce the communication".

I ♥ my labels.

FIGURE 60: Ending headlines with periods may irritate and alienate readers.

FIGURE 61: All sans serif, widely spaced lines, reversed out of strong green, picking up tones of green from the photograph. The watch is gold. Not a great reading environment for perhaps 95 per cent of readers.

Out, damned spot!

Many advertising typographers place a full stop or period at the end of their headings. No newspaper typographers do. The thinking is that editorial headlines in newspapers and magazines rarely form sentences, and therefore don't need full stops, but advertising headlines frequently form sentences, and therefore require periods. Advertising copywriters also see the full point as adding emphasis.

Does the full stop have an effect on readers' comprehension, and if so, is that effect significant? A study was conducted in Sydney between December, 1986, and March, 1987, at the request of David Ogilvy.

Magazine pages were created in the Ayer No. 1 format with a slightly less than half page horizontal illustration, with a headline below it, and the text below again, like David Ogilvy's Rolls-Royce ad. (figure 3, p.18). Four different pages were printed, with each design being in two formats — one with the headline full-stopped, the other without.

The content of two of the designs was editorial with a tourism theme, and of the other two advertising, with a motoring theme — adaptations of the Ogilvy Rolls-Royce advertisement.

Results

There were no significant differences between the individual designs in levels of comprehension. There were, however, differences in comprehension between the headlines with periods and those in editorial style, without.

Table 20: Comprehension of advertisements with or without a period (full stop) at the end of the headline.

Comprehension level	Good	Fair	Poor
Headline without a period	71	19	10
Headline with a period	58	22	20

Comments

After the project was completed, the members of the sample were questioned on their reactions to the material. Those who read the headlines with full stops were conscious of the punctuation mark and commented on it.

FIGURE 63 (below): A nice layout from TIME Magazine. Gravity and type choices good, but spoilt by the bastard measure with ragged setting introduced into two columns wrapping around the illustration at the bottom of the page.

FIGURE 62 (above): Full page ad. Everything in sans serif capitals, full stops in the headline, body text small, light and reversed out of black across the full width of the page, contact information is small, light caps — in grey. Did King Furniture expect people to read the text? The question: will that "look" sell better than easily-read text would do?

- Twenty-two percent of the total sample said they realized they were reading an advertisement when they came to the period, even though they were not at that point aware of the content. Interestingly, 10 per cent of the sample indicated this discovery diminished their intention to concentrate on reading the material.
- Twelve per cent of the sample indicated that they found the use of the full stops unnatural, and wondered why they had been used. Six per cent of the sample said the full stop indicated to them that there was no need to read any more of the message. All that needed to be said had been said.

Conclusion

In this study, 13 per cent fewer readers displayed good comprehension when full stops were used.

The reasons for this were:

- The full stop tends to pull some readers up with a jerk, and indicate to them there is no need to read on.
- The full stop is, to some readers, an indication that what follows is advertising material, and, in their minds, not as consequential as if it were editorial.

The conclusion is that the use of full stops at the end of headlines in advertisements which include a considerable amount (50 per cent) of reading matter, may have a detrimental effect on readers' comprehension.

Only two per cent of the sample were aware of the subtle distinction that editorial headlines rarely include verbs, and that advertising headlines frequently do.

Note: The method used did not permit testing of advertisements which relied only on a headline without supporting text. Logically, the full stop in these circumstances would have little or no effect on comprehension.

Widows, jumps and bastard measure

Throughout the program, readers were asked to express opinions on minor typographical elements, such as whether widows (lines of type of less than full length at the head of a column) annoyed them; their reactions when asked to jump from one page to another to continue an article; whether they found extremely narrow or extremely wide measure body type easy to read; whether reversed body type was acceptable; and the value of cross headings.

The results were calculated, and are expressed here as percentages.

Current newspapers and magazines were used to exemplify the elements being discussed.

Design elements

- Sixty-one per cent of readers said that jumps, where an article is continued on a later page, or on several later pages in successive jumps, were annoying.
- Sixty-six per cent said they disliked pages which had large headlines with two or three paragraphs of copy, followed by an exhortation to jump to a later page. This was particularly disliked when the article was found to be inconsequential, such as an injury to a jockey's armpit, or merely a newspaper promotional stunt.
- Eighty-three per cent said they usually did not follow jumps. This may not concern advertising people — but what if their advertisement is on a jump page? It will need to be brilliant to be read!
- Thirty-nine per cent said that if they were convinced to jump to continue reading an article, they frequently discovered they had not returned to where they were originally reading.
- Sixty-seven per cent said they preferred illustrations to carry a description, such as a caption. The practice of some publications of describing an illustration in an accompanying article was frequently criticized.
- Eighty-one per cent said they found special screening effects on illustrations such as mezzo, circular line or horizontal line, to be annoying. Some said they thought the screens a device intended to disguise a poor illustration — or a printer's mistake!
- Seventy-seven per cent said articles in which body type jumped over an illustration or cutoff heading, contrary to the natural flow of reading, annoyed them. The natural expectation was that once a barrier such as an illustration or cutoff was reached, the article would be continued at the head of the next leg of type.

The moral is clear: it is not difficult to annoy readers, either by commission or omission. And the message is also clear: before the editor or designer inserts a typographical element, he or she should think hard about the effect it may have on readers.

Headlines

- Fifty-seven per cent said they disliked "screamer" headlines, such as are used on the front pages of some popular tabloid newspapers, and in some large display advertisements, because they had to hold the newspaper or magazine further than usual from the eyes to be able to read the type. The criterion for annoyance was the need to focus twice to read the entire content (see figure 64, p.100). Perhaps this is the dynamic behind *Screamer headlines might not be read!* (p.131).
- Multi-deck headlines were generally disliked. Fifty-six per cent indicated they found headlines of more than four decks difficult to comprehend.
- Sixty-eight per cent said they became bored with long, wordy headlines. The comment was made frequently that there seemed to be nothing left to read after the headline. This is introspective — but the warning is valid and ought not to be ignored.

Body type

- Thirty-eight per cent of readers found body type set wider than about 60 characters hard to read. A further 22 per cent indicated they probably wouldn't read wide measure body type even though they didn't find any difficulty reading it. *Note that the measure is by the number of characters, not a fixed number of picas, inches or centimeters. Obviously, the bigger the type, the longer the acceptable line length and vice versa, within the limits of preferred type sizes* (see table 21 and figure 72, p.112, for type size preferences).
- Eighty-seven per cent said they found extremely narrow measures, such as less than 20 characters, hard to read.
- Seventy-eight per cent indicated they found cross headings useful, particularly in long articles. None said they found cross headings unattractive or intrusive.
- None said they were offended by — or even were aware of — widows (As the definition of a widow varies, we are considering here a short line which ends a paragraph, and which is turned to the top of the adjoining column. In practice, the widow has the effect of forcing the reader to continue to the next column). In fact, some direct marketers and other business writers deliberately break sentences across pages or columns to drag the reader on. Apparently only printers, editors and designers are offended!

- Only seven per cent of readers said they found body matter set in capitals easy to read. Readers were shown text set in 9 point Univers over 13 picas (2⅙ inches or 5 centimeters) width to a depth of 20 centimeters (8 inches). A central section 5 centimeters (2 inches) deep was set in capitals, and readers were asked to indicate if they found this section easy to read. An overwhelming 93 per cent said "no". They were then shown similar material set to the same dimensions in Corona light, a serif face. The results were identical. When similar material was presented entirely in Univers lower case, 22 per cent said they found it easy to read. With Corona lower case 100 per cent said they found it easy to read. (Note: compared these expressions of preference with the reading comprehension results, table 3 [p.47]. They are very much in the same direction.)

FIGURE 64: *An archetypal screaming tabloid headline! Readers resent ads which mimic this style.*

FIGURE 65: A eggy yellow (PMS 138 perhaps) printed on two screens of the same colour. In addition to very limited contrast, the reader has to deal with the light weight of a sans serif face in small size.

FACT FILES

SOUTH AMERICAN FESTIVAL

Where: Bondi Pavilion
Community Cultural Centre
When: 20 February 2005
Cost: around $20, tickets are available
at the door. Children under the
age of 12 get in free
Contact: (02) 8362 3400 or
visit www.waverley.nsw.gov.au

VIVA SPAIN

Where: 315 Victoria Street, Melbourne
When: open 10am–6pm, Tuesday to Friday
and 9am–2pm Saturday. Classes
usually start around 6.30pm or 7pm.
Bookings are essential
Cost: around $65 for a three-hour
tapas-tasting and language class
Contact: (03) 9329 0485, www.vivaspain.com.au

NEW NORCIA

Where: 132km from Perth, WA
When: tours leave the New Norcia Museum

FIGURE 66: All caps reversed out of textured green, not a lot of leading (interlinear space), ragged left. Readability about zero. Luckily it's a very short message, but even then …

We want to say 'thank you' for the great welcome you gave us to Mordialloc.

Just a year ago, we nervously opened the door of our little Fresh Gourmet Poultry shop in Mordialloc.

We had been blown away by the delicious La Ionica chicken, we had worked out great prices, but did you want that?

Great welcome!

We need not have worried. We had a wonderful tin as you came in, saw how good our chicken looke took some home and found it delicious, then cam back for more! *And* to talk about good food, chicken recipes, marinades and sauces.

So now we are happily celebrating Mordialloc Fresh Gourmet Poultry's 1st anniversary.

Surprise! Great prices!

We're also happy to see how surprised you were by that prices!

The secret is simple. We are exactly what you see, a family business, our little shop, and the three of us behind the counter — Annette, Sarah and Helen.

When you buy from us you are buying our chic not paying for an army of suits in plush offices of company cars, and millions in TV advertisin

Happy anniversary! FREE chicken!*

To thank you for the great welcomed you have given us, and to celebrate our 1st Anniversary, we are offering you FREE snack-size samples of our delicious marinaded chicken products.

When you come into our shop to buy, we will add a sample of a different fresh, marinaded chicken for you to take home and try. FREE! (*Offer ends Sat. 21/9/02)

So Happy Anniversary! *Please turn over to learn more about our delicious, chemical-free chicken...*

Annotation callouts:

Headline at the head for best reading gravity.

Illustrations at top right and bottom left. Good gravity.

Human faces, eyes, to grab readers' eyes and direct them to the starting point.

Headline and sub-heads printed dull red to attract attention but minimize interference in reading.

Body text in Galliard; an excellent serif face which encourages readers to read.

READ THIS FLYER!

Why don't they read your inserts?

In 1988, a major Australian organization decided to produce a leaflet to be inserted into newspapers and magazines. It called in an advertising agency, and commissioned a one-color leaflet for a long print run. But somewhere along the track, between the creative spark and the reader, the wheels fell off.

The leaflet had a headline on the front, and two pages of text on the inside. When the leaflet was subjected to a readership research study, it was found that only nine per cent of readers displayed good comprehension, twenty nine per cent fair comprehension, and a whopping sixty two per cent, poor comprehension. In effect, only one reader in ten had much idea of what the leaflet was about — and that figure was of those who actually took the trouble to read it.

Now in figure 69 (p.106) you may notice a couple of questionable typographic features. First, the leaflet was set in sans serif type.

A considerable body of research, including this study, shows that while sans serif may be clean cut, modern, authoritative, decisive, sharp and exciting — these are all creative department adjectives — it is notoriously difficult to read in continuous text.

Second, the leaflet was a headless wonder. David Ogilvy, who knew about these matters, railed against them, and Professor Siegfried Vogele, Dean of the Institute of Direct Marketing in Munich, has used his eye-camera technique to show how they fail. The eye-camera is used to time and track the eye movements of readers when they come upon a printed spread. It has been invaluable in determining how people look at and read pages of text and illustrations.

What he found is illustrated in figure 68 (p.104). When a potential reader comes upon a spread, the eyes alight at the top right corner; possibly because this is the first point exposed when a leaflet is opened or a newspaper or magazine page turned. From this point at the top right corner the eyes

FIGURE 67 (left): A letterbox flyer in two colours, black and a dull red. Its layout, type and ink choices encourage recipients to read it and to be persuaded.

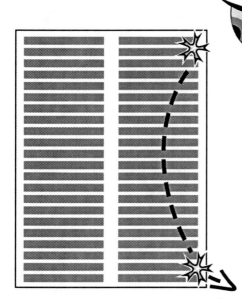

FIGURE 68: Eye movements on entering a page typical of those recorded by Professor Vogele's eye tracking camera for left to right readers. They do a quick scan as shown, then move to upper left to begin reading … if they have seen something they like. (Book readers, of course, just continue reading.)

68a (left): No display, no fixes within the page, no incentive to go back and read, thus no message gets through. The reader is in and out of the page with just a shallow sweep from the entry point to exit.

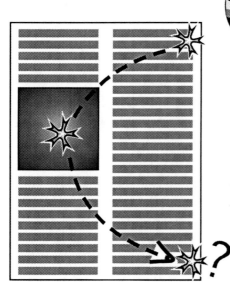

68b (left): A display item catches the eye and takes it further into the page, raising the chance that the reader will see something of interest and return to the top to read.

68c (right): Numerous display items catch the eye and make for a slow, complex path over the page. This sort of initial exploration is highly likely to result in reading of the page. The top left headline ensures good gravity as reading begins.

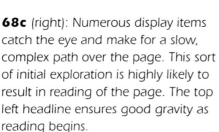

make a parabolic sweep to the left and then back and down to the right, sending messages to the brain when they make a fix on display elements. At the end of that sweep the brain makes a decision, based on the number or magnitude of the fixes, whether there is enough incentive to read the spread.

If there is good display, such as a headline and an illustration on the left side of the spread, the sweep is extended towards those design elements. As the eyes track onwards, they're able to make fixes on other display elements on the way (see figure 68b and 68c). All these fixes have an accumulated effect on the subconscious, and help to reinforce the decision, when the sweep is completed, about whether to go back and read or not.

But what if there are minimal display elements, or none at all?

The parabolic sweep then becomes a very shallow curve, almost straight to the bottom of the page. No display, no fixes for the eyes, no messages to the brain, no incentive to read, no response to the message (figure 68a).

Our headless leaflet (figure 69) includes two display elements, both negative in terms of easy reading: underlining and the increased interlinear space (10 point on a 20 point body). The latter held the dubious record of being design flavor of the year for the more than five years (have we mentioned before that odd typesetting elements like this fall in and out of favor with designers — and that some of them persist for years against all logic and in the case of advertising, results?). This device slows down reading. Slower reading results in reduced comprehension, reduced comprehension means boredom, and boredom means readers won't be getting the message and buying the product the leaflet is promoting!

The "owner" of the leaflet decided to try a novel approach.

The interlinear spacing was reduced, the type set in a serif face. Without using any more space, without dropping a word of the text, a headline, cross-headings and an illustration were placed in the spread as shown in figure 70, p.107).

The effect? The leaflet was submitted to the same research study as the earlier one. The level of good comprehension leaped from nine to 37 per cent, fair comprehension rose from 29 to 48 per cent, and most importantly, the level of poor comprehension — those who really did not get the message — dropped from 62 per cent to 15 per cent.

This result suggested further research into some of the questions that arose. A further 24 different leaflets were subjected to a study involving a sample of 15,000 readers.

Australia's motorists will pay the Federal Government a whopping $6.5 billion in fuel taxes this year.

Last year, only personal income tax earned more revenue for the Federal Government.

Every time a driver stops at a petrol station, half the money he spends on patrol goes to the Government.

Which means petrol, a necessity, attracts 150 per cent tax. While "luxuries" such as jewellery, cosmetics and hi-fi equipment attract 30 per cent tax.

Where does the revenue from petrol tax go?

Not where it should. Less than 20 per cent of this Federal tax is spent on Australia's roads.

After allowing for inflation, the amount the Federal Government is spending on roads is 25 per cent less than it was three years ago.

Because roads require regular maintenance, State Road authorities are having to spend 40 percent of their available funds keeping them in reasonable shape.

However, this percentage is presently rising, leaving less each year for the development and extension of the nation's road network.,

As a result, traffic in our major cities is grinding to a half.

Vehicles spend up to one third of urban road running time just standing still, wasting fuel.

Rough roads, both in the city and country, increase fuel consumption by up to 20 percent and vehicle repair costs by 36 per cent.

Poor roads also contribute to crashes, which last year cost the community $5,700 million.

Better roads save lives

Replacing a two-lane road with a freeway, for instance, can reduce crashes by up to 85 per cent.

Australians rely on their roads.

Over 97 per cent of passenger travel is on the nation's roads.

Nearly 83 per cent of domestic tourist travel is by road, as is 43 per cent of travel between capital cities by visiting international tourists.

Adding to the problem is the expectation that Australians will increase their use of the road network considerably over the next decade.

The number of cars and station wagons estimated to be using the roads by the end of the century will be 30 per cent higher than today.

The amount of freight carried will increase by two-thirds.

You don't have to put up with bad roads.

If you think a grater share of the fuel taxes you pay should be spent on roads, talk to peopled about it.

Write to your newspaper. Tell your radio talkback show. Best of all, let your Federal MP or the Federal Minister for Transport and Communications know how you feel.

Tell them all that a grater share of the Federal petrol tax you pay should be spent on our roads.

FIGURE 69: A leaflet with minimal display elements. A glance tells you the alternative with display elements is much more reader-friendly.

Show them how angry you are

Australia's motorists will pay the Federal Government a whopping $6.5 billion in fuel taxes this year.

Last year, only personal income tax earned more revenue for the Federal Government.

Every time a driver stops at a petrol station, half the money he spends on patrol goes to the Government.

Which means petrol, a necessity, attracts 150 per cent tax. While "luxuries" such as jewellery, cosmetics and hi-fi equipment attract 30 per cent tax.

Not where it should. Less than 20 percent of this Federal tax is spent on Australia's roads.

After allowing for inflation, the amount the Federal Government is spending on roads is 25 per cent less than it was three years ago.

Because roads require regular maintenance, State Road authorities are having to spend 40 percent of their available funds keeping them in reasonable shape.

Grinding to a halt

However, this percentage is presently rising, leaving less each year for the development and extension of the nation's road network.,

As a result, traffic in our major cities is grinding to a halt.

Vehicles spend up to one third of urban road running time just standing still, wasting fuel.

Rough roads, both in the city and country, increase fuel consumption by up to 20 per cent and vehicle repair costs by 36 per cent. Poor roads also contribute to crashes,

which last year cost the community $5,700 million. Better roads save lives. Replacing a two-lane road with a freeway, for instance, can reduce crashes by up to 85 per cent.

Australians rely on their roads; over 97 per cent of passenger travel is on the nation's roads, nearly 83 percent of domestic tourist travel is by road, as is 43 per cent of travel between capital cities by visiting international tourists.

Adding to the problem is the expectation that Australians will increase their use of the road network considerably over the next decade. The number of cars and station wagons estimated to be using the roads by the end of the century will be 30 per cent higher than today. The amount of freight carried will increase by two-thirds.

Who to write to

If you think a grater share of the fuel taxes you pay should be spent on roads, talk to people about it.

Write to your newspaper. Tell your radio talkback show. Best of all, let your Federal MP or the Federal Minister for Transport and Communications know how you feel.

Tell them all that a grater share of the Federal petrol tax you pay should be spent on our roads.

FIGURE 70: The same information with more readable type and display elements added to guide the reader's eyes.

What we learned

The questions that arose, and the answers to them:

1. To what extent do people read leaflets?

Leaflets distributed indiscriminately into letterboxes had an average readership of about five per cent. The best result was 10 per cent; the worst, one per cent.

2. What were the strike rates if the leaflets were targeted?

Considerably better. The average readership was 25 per cent. The best result was 33 per cent; the worst, eight per cent.

3. Was there a difference if the leaflets were inserted in a magazine?

Yes there was. The results were considerably better than gratuitous distribution, but less than a targeted leaflet. The average result was 12 per cent, with the best 33 per cent and the worst five per cent.

4. Is the number of words on a leaflet significant?

In a word, no. David Ogilvy says his experience is that long advertising copy generally sells better than short copy. Given a relevant topic, people will read long leaflets as much as they will read short ones. (There are many factors affecting whether people will read long copy, ranging from whether they are skilled readers to the degree of personal involvement and/or risk there is in the product or service being offered to them.)

5. What importance do illustrations have in a leaflet and are photographs more, or less effective, than art?

We know from Professor Vogele's research that illustrations have a part to play in getting readers' attention by supplying fixes for the eyes on that first sweep. We also know that illustrations can help to reinforce a message contained in headlines or text (Ogilvy's Rolls-Royce advertisement is an excellent example). We are not able to forge a research link between recall and intention to buy or act on a message, and in the type of leaflet we are considering recall is probably all we have to go on.

What emerged in the study was that photographs were recalled far more clearly than art work by more than half of those who read the leaflets. This is consistent with psychological research using the eye camera which shows that the human face is the strongest magnet to the human eye and that from very early in life, the photograph of the face beats a drawing of it. (Figure 67 [p.102] uses this factor to reinforce the headline.)

6. David Ogilvy says that in advertisements, five times as many people read headlines as read body copy. Is there any parallel with leaflets?

Yes there is — in spades. The study showed that, irrespective of the topic, style or method of distribution, about half of the sample of 15,000 people, one in two of them, read the headlines of *all* the leaflets they received. Most of them read no further.

This tells us something very important. It tells us that if we put our message in the headline, half of our target audience has a chance of getting that message. And if they find the headline message compelling, we just might induce them to read on, find out a little more about what we are telling or selling them, and take the next step, buy.

7. We know that 50 per cent of our target are likely to read our headline. But are they going to understand it?

The study went a step further by finding out how many of those who read the headlines actually knew what those headlines meant. The results were frightening. Here's a case in point:

In Victoria, Australia, when random breath testing of drivers was introduced to detect alcohol, the traffic authority ran a very successful educational campaign under the slogan 'Don't Blow Your Licence'. In neighboring New South Wales (NSW), the campaign director thought that slogan was too cumbersome — he wanted something snappier. He determined it should be simply 'Don't Blow It'. This became the headline on the NSW leaflet and posters.

But when the comprehensibility of this was researched, it was found that 100 per cent of those who read the headline 'Don't Blow Your Licence' understood precisely what it meant, but only four per cent of those who read 'Don't Blow It' could explain what the headline attempted to convey. Some of the respondents thought the leaflets were advocating civil disobedience by refusing to blow into the test equipment!

So the answer is: use the headline to support the text, give the eyes something to fix on, and make sure it carries the message.

8. Is the type size important, and if it is, what is the optimum size or range of sizes for leaflets?

Four thousand members of the research study sample took part in a further test to determine preferred type sizes for discretionary reading. A table and chart of the full results are presented over the page (p.110).

Readers were given samples and asked to nominate their choices from

Readers' preferred type sizes

Table 21: Readers' type size and setting preferences. Percentages of reader preferences expressed.

Type size & leading	Pref. %		
8 point set solid 8/8	14	12 point set solid 12/12	72
8 point set 8/9	21	12 point set 12/13	90
8 point set 8/10	26	12 point set 12/14	82
9 point set solid 9/9	63	13 point set solid 13/13	66
9 point set 9/10	66	13 point set 13/14	70
9 point set 9/11	71	13 point set 13/15	68
10 point set solid 10/10	69	14 point set solid 14/14	59
10 point set 10/11	86	14 point set 14/15	61
10 point set 10/12	92	14 point set 14/16	63
11 point set solid 11/11	77	15 point set solid 15/15	21
11 point set 11/12	93	15 point set 15/16	25
11 point set 11/13	98	15 point set 15/17	28

FIGURE 72: The graphic format leaves no doubt about the cluster of preferred type sizes from 9 point to 14 point and the preference for a point or two of interlineal space (leading). This would vary with different faces as sizes of type and 'natural' spacing vary for a given point size, but the preferred cluster is quite clear and ought not to be ignored.

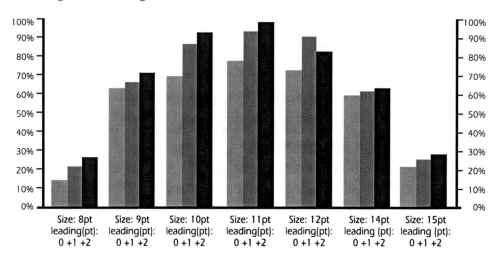

a range of sizes they found easy to read in natural setting with no extra interlinear space (leading). There was a clear preferred range, from nine point to 14 point (table 21, opposite), with 11 point regarded as the easiest to read by 77 per cent of the sample; 12 point by 72 per cent; 10 point by 69 per cent; 13 point by 66 per cent, and 9 point, a common newspaper size, by 63 per cent.

But when one or two points of interlinear space were introduced, the ease of reading increased considerably.

Four results stand out with approval from nine out of ten or better of those sampled: 11 point type on 13 point body (11/13 point) preferred by a whopping 98 per cent of the sample; 11/12 point, 93 per cent; 10/12 point, 92 per cent; and 12 /13 point, 90 per cent (table 21, opposite).

Readers made a clear distinction between type set natural or solid, with no added interlinear space (leading), with which they did not feel comfortable, and type set with one or two points of interlinear space added with which they did feel comfortable.

While readers could not tell why, most said they preferred the text with the extra leading between the lines.

A closer look at the sample showed that subjects who, in the course of business or leisure, were avid readers generally preferred one point additional interlinear spacing, while those who were less practised readers generally preferred two points of extra space. (Note how this ties in with the extra spacing between lines needed by those who are not fluent or mature readers. Figure 93, p.151, and figure 94, p.152, refer.)

There is a clear preferred size bracket for text type — starting at 9 points and heading up to 14 points. Above and below those two, preference crashes. Three points are worth noting:

- Many newspapers use 8 point type, but it is always with at least one point of interlinear space. Newspapers get away with using this small type because they select fonts with a good 'x height', so they are perceived as relatively large for their point size, and the information they carry is high on their readers' 'wanted lists'. Readers will put up with a non-preferred font for the sake of the subject matter.
- As indicated above, there is considerable variation in the perceived and actual size of the same point size in different fonts. Obviously, this means that selection of type for any given task should take such variation into account and table 21 should be used as a general guide rather than a set of hard and fast rules. A possible research direction

would be looking at these preferences in different print environments, such as magazines, newspapers, books and letters.

To summarize:

- Leaflet design and contents should accommodate known reading traits and idiosyncrasies rather than ignore them, or even worse, try to change them.
- Headlines should contain sufficient of the message to be able to stand on their own — as they frequently have to do.
- Teasing or intriguing headlines, unless they state the message clearly, may fail.
- Where possible, leaflets should contain illustrations and a headline on both the cover and inside pages to support the message and entice the reader to scan … and then to read on.

FIGURE 71: *All capitals and worse — most of it is oblique sans serif! Printed in dull green on white (low contrast), but there's no problem with type size!*

The research showed high levels of comprehension among those reading articles which were designed simply, and which took into consideration the physiology of reading and the linearity of the Latin alphabet; with the body set fully justified in black serif type; and with headlines set natural and printed in black ink.

It must be emphasized that these parameters don't necessarily equate with dullness of design. Exciting concepts with a high degree of comprehensibility — editorial or advertising — can be achieved with a little thought as is shown in numerous examples in any magazine or newspaper you leaf through. Unfortunately, the same scan through often uncovers examples where it is clear a lot of thought and effort has gone into producing a low degree of comprehensibility!

The designer should analyze every element he or she puts into a page. If it helps reading rhythm, keep it; if it doesn't, its value is questionable; if it works against comprehension, it should be eliminated.

The negative aspects of typography illuminated in this book should give the designer considerable food for thought.

- Thirty-eight per cent of readers showed poor comprehension when reading layouts which forced the eye to fight against reading gravity.
- Sixty-five per cent showed poor comprehension of articles set in sans serif body type.
- Forty per cent showed poor comprehension of articles set ragged on the right, and seventy two per cent showed poor comprehension of articles set ragged on the left.
- Sixty-five per cent showed poor comprehension of articles with high chroma color headings.
- Eighty-one per cent showed poor comprehension of text printed in bright process colors.
- Eighty-eight per cent showed poor comprehension of articles printed in reverse.

While it is not suggested that the findings of this study can be extrapolated to every typographical situation, they do suggest that if the intention is to communicate information and ideas rather than play with shapes and pretty colors, more attention should be paid to:

- The consideration of the physical burden which reading a newspaper, magazine, or advertisement places on the reader.
- An awareness of the physiology of reading and an acceptance that design *must* accommodate it, not try to ignore or change it.
- The inescapable fact is that a brilliant piece of graphic design which goes unread is a waste of paper, ink, money and effort, and perhaps above all, a lost opportunity to communicate.

Do the sums! If your job is communication, isn't it better to communicate with a million people using a design that rates perhaps five out of 10 for artistic brilliance, than to produce a scintillating design that rates a 10 out of 10, yet reaches only half the people?

FIGURE 73: *Minimalist, ultra-modern design, but given that it flouts the type and layout rules, the question must be asked whether something more conventional would actually sell more product. Do they seriously think the text, minimal though it is, will be read? Colour is minimal, but the brightest spot is at bottom right corner (red and yellow shapes) which tends to drag the eye away.*

APPLYING THE RULES

Fifteen cases

By Geoffrey Heard

Colin Wheildon's research shows that the difference between good reader comprehension and reader disaster can be a fine line — and is often the opposite of the design trend-of-the-day.

In this section, we look at 15 advertisements, flyers and pages, point to weaknesses and strengths, and suggest changes to some to bring them into line with the research results.

Some are minor matters, some are gross. Some very good looking pages are clearly at fault from a reader comprehension perspective. Figure 74 overleaf is a classic case. Looks fantastic; reads like hell! Some other pages are just plain ugly, and fight readers too!

Note that in all of these cases, as with other examples shown in this book, we are not claiming omniscience, but rather, we are bringing to bear the results of research. We do not say that advertisements set out as suggested here will sell better every time than the way they were set out originally. We are simply saying that Colin Wheildon's research suggests that readers have definite preferences for certain type faces and layouts, so if we want people to read and comprehend our editorial, advertisements, flyers, leaflets, letters, circulars, brochures and reports, if our primary message is in the words, we ought to be putting out the welcome mat to readers by providing them with their preferred reading environment.

Colin Wheildon's research provides the baseline rules of thumb. It is often said that rules are made to be broken — and fair enough too — but if you are breaking them, you need to be monitoring to be sure that your different way is a *better* way of achieving your goal, rather than just a pretty looking mighty step backwards.

Type right, gravity right, but ...

Excellent reading gravity, good choice of type faces but ...

The whole reversed out of a blue-grey background. The moment we see that, we know reader comprehension of the message must plummet. In this case, the designer has added insult to injury by making the background a gradient, lightening it to the equivalent of about a 20 per cent screen at the bottom of the columns.

Colin Wheildon did not research this refinement of reversed out type torture, but the reader doesn't need to be told. As the eyes move down the first column and hit the light area, they are jumping around all over the place.

FIGURE 74: Eew! For the eyes, this is on the nose!

Westlawn: lower case headline

This is a direct response advertisement found in a sailing magazine. You can be sure it is earning its keep — it is very easy to keep tabs on performance when you are advertising for calls and mail. Just count.

As it stands (below left) it is a simple layout with good reading gravity. But would it pull better with some minor changes to layout and type choices? Worth a try!

At right is the result of a quick make-over using the words and elements available as is. Headline changed to lower case, body type switched from sans to serif (Caslon) and justified, picture flopped to 'point' readers back into the copy and leave the wrap area as ragged right rather than ragged left *and* right.

Since the coupon is on the left side of the layout, this ad. should always be placed on the outside of a left-hand page. If a right-hand placement is available, then the layout ought to be changed to switch the coupon to that side. People don't like to cut into the page for a coupon.

FIGURE 75: Original (left) and make-over (right). This study shows us small things can make a big difference, so let's get them right..

LEARN YACHT DESIGN AT WESTLAWN

For more than 70 years, Westlawn has educated many of the world's finest boat and yacht designers. You'll learn at home, at your own pace, to design new sailboats and powerboats or modify existing ones. When you graduate, you'll have the top-level skills you need to launch your career in a yacht design firm, a production boat manufacturing company or even to establish your own design office. To learn more about Westlawn and our unique home study program, call or write for our FREE illustrated course catalog today.

WESTLAWN

Westlawn Institute of Marine Technology
733 Summer Street, Suite CW, Stamford, CT 06901
PH: 203.359.0500 www.westlawn.org

800-836-2059
24 Hour Toll Free

Please send me your FREE illustrated catalog. I understand there is no obligation and no salesman will call.

NAME _____

ADDRESS _____

CITY _____

STATE _____ ZIP _____

COUNTRY _____

- Not-for-profit educational affiliate of the American Boat and Yacht Council.
- Accredited member of the Distance Education and Training Council.
- Approved by the Connecticut Commissioner of Higher Education.
- Founded in 1930.

Learn yacht design at Westlawn

For more than 70 years, Westlawn has educated many of the world's finest boat and yacht designers. You'll learn at home, at your own pace, to design new sailboats and powerboats or modify existing ones. When you graduate, you'll have the top-level skills you need to launch your career in a yacht design firm, a production boat manufacturing company or even to establish your own design office. To learn more about Westlawn and our unique home study program, call or write for our FREE illustrated course catalog today.

WESTLAWN

Westlawn Institute of Marine Technology
733 Summer Street, Suite CW, Stamford, CT 06901
PH: 203.359.0500 www.westlawn.org

800-836-2059
24 Hour Toll Free

Please send me your FREE illustrated catalog. I understand there is no obligation and no salesman will call.

NAME _____

ADDRESS _____

CITY _____

STATE _____ ZIP _____

COUNTRY _____

- Not-for-profit educational affiliate of the American Boat and Yacht Council.
- Accredited member of the Distance Education and Training Council.
- Approved by the Connecticut Commissioner of Higher Education.
- Founded in 1930.

It works! Just change the body type

An advertisement from Readers' Digest. In this case, the words really do matter — they are meant to be read and understood. Reading gravity is good. The dull orange used for the headline is not overly intrusive; neither is the touch of blue in the "investor" at the foot.

The only problem for the reader is the condensed sans serif type, Helvetica, set near solid. Readers would prefer a serif type and possibly a point more leading.

FIGURE 75: So near …

Life prescription

Another direct response advertisement, this time a flyer for letterboxing or insertion in a local newspaper or magazine. As before, the make-over uses the words and elements used in the original.

FIGURE 77: A letterboxed flyer.

77a: The original (right) has so much red it loses its impact. Hard selling testimonials over two colors are difficult to read.

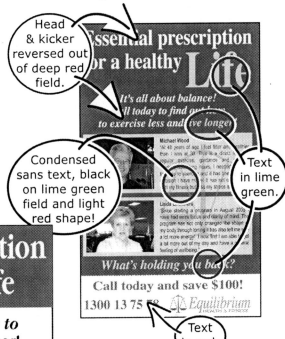

77b: The remake (left) limits type reversed out of red to the head and bottom kicker. Linking two testimonials to the balance shape in a light screen of red builds accord between the text and the layout (but also test the ad. without the shape — if it interferes with reading, drop it!). This also provides more space for the testimonials so they can be set in a slightly larger, serif type with reasonable leading for easier reading.

FIGURE 78: *A design aimed at designers. Is the design more important than the written message? In this case — probably!*

Blue & green should never be seen ...

That saying might have been true once, but the two go together now! The problem with this full page magazine advertisement — in blue and green — is not the choice of colors but the type which has been reversed out of them.

The headline as a circle in all caps reversed out of a green gradient background with shapes. You can't read the headline at a glance, of course, but you can read it. It is saved by the green chosen, it is a fairly low chroma color, and the weight of the type. It also helps that the word "green" and the background are in accord with each other.

The same cannot be said of the bottom half of the ad. The strikes against easy reading and good comprehension:

- The text is set in a fairly light weight of a sans serif type face.
- The kicker is set three decks deep in all caps.
- The lines are too long for comfortable reading. Two columns would have been better with this page and type size combination.
- The whole is reversed out of a high chroma blue.

In addition to simply breaking the rule that large amounts of text should not be reversed out of *any* color, the designer here has fallen into a further trap — the used of light type with fine lines in multicolor printing. If the blue were a spot color this text would have been difficult to read, but because it is made up of two colors, cyan and magenta, and registration is not perfect vertically, it is even more difficult! The vertical parts of the letters are white, the horizontal parts are cyan — seen here as a lighter gray.

The message is (and always has been): if you *must* reverse type out of a color, do it out of a solid color for preference and in all cases, choose a type weight which will not succumb to problems like poor registration and ink spread.

A saving grace in this case is that this advertisement was in a magazine for designers and was directed towards designers. Thus it might be expected that the *design* is the most important selling element here; the actual words might have been quite secondary — more important as a design element than for their meaning. The words themselves lend weight to this argument. Read the all caps kicker; it doesn't make a lot of sense.

More blue & green

In this case, we are looking at a light weight of sans serif type, Helvetica, reversed out of a light lime green — quite a high chroma color. Contrast is very low and the message is quite difficult to read. Add to that the centered type and the fact that there is a play on words which doesn't actually make sense — and the reader is lost, hit by a triple whammy!

(The play on words: the answer to the question "How far would you go …" is *not* "just around the corner". BP Ultimate is not available that widely.)

It is worth noting that difficulties in reading and comprehending a message are cumulative. Psychologists have shown that adding interfering factors to a reading task diverts readers and slashes reading speed.

A technical note: in this case, at least five colors were used in printing; the high chroma lime green is a spot color, not a four color composite, so at least the type shapes retained their integrity.

FIGURE 79: *Almost a disappearing headline.*

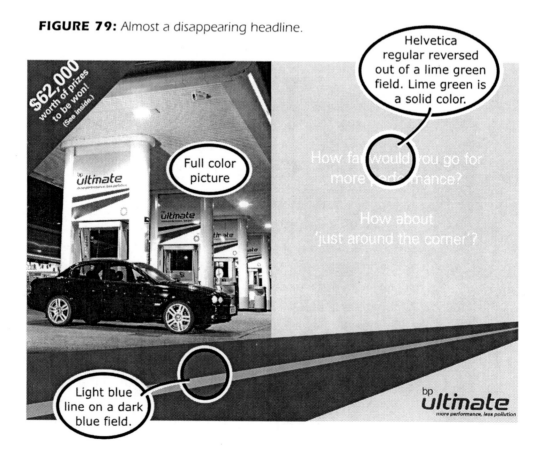

Making space for good type and more impact

This A4 (21 x 29.7 cm; 8.25 x 11.7 in.) flyer printed on quality glossy paper features a full color photograph bleeding on three sides with shades of mainly dark blue in the background, a dark blue band across the foot and all type reversed out. It was delivered as a two fold DL dropped into a magazine.

By shifting the elements around we can:

- Make space for the body copy to be printed in easy-to-read black on white.
- Present a much stronger selling message when the flyer is folded.
- Reduce the size of the document by a third for significant paper savings making it a single fold to DL size.

FIGURE 80: Two fold DL flyer.

80a: The flyer as received — folded (top) and fully open (lower).

80b: Makeover uses strong reversed type for the head and kicker but black on white for the body — and ends up with space savings and a stronger presentation overall. (We're selling eyewear, right? So let's see the eyes!). Folded format (top) and open (lower).

FIGURE 81: Layout, type choices and background field all make the message difficult to comprehend. The situation is further confused by the words themselves.

Are they serious?

You have to ask the question when you see a full page advertisement like this. The headline, in a dinky font reversed out of black at the bottom of the text, is a play on words (sigh!) which like a previous ad. actually doesn't make a lot of sense. If you can find your way to the body text, you will struggle to read it — it is set black on dark brown with light brown shapes through it dragging the eyes hither and thither.

After reading the text, you will read it again; you may think that in the clutter you have missed something. No you haven't! They *didn't* say what they were actually talking about.

Perhaps it is one of those things like a Rolls-Royce — if you need to ask the price, you can't afford one. In this case, if you need to ask what they are selling — a card, an escort service, a resort, a string of resorts, a spy service ("We know you've arrived" — another play on words?), you are not the prospective purchaser they are addressing.

Presumably, this advertisement reflects someone's notion of richness and luxury. It might be suggested that advertisements which are as difficult to penetrate as this one are more likely to make the magazine owner rich than the advertiser.

A magazine page that works for readers

Good reading gravity and good type choices allow some departures from "best practise" without impacting too much on readability as this page from *Business Week* shows.

FIGURE 82: A good looking page that can be easily read and understood.

And one that's not so good

Business Week obviously wants its readers to read and comprehend complex information; looking at some pop culture magazine pages, it is a fair question to ask whether mature readers are the target audience.

FIGURE 83: Reading nasties mean skilled readers suffer, but perhaps they are not the target market for this pop culture mag.

Meant to be read

A well laid out page with good gravity, good type selection, but …

FIGURE 84: The page started with good gravity and good type selection. But there is no need for ragged right instead of justified text and the graphic under the text in tones of pink and green made reading the black text more than difficult. The full size section gives an indication of the degree of difficulty.

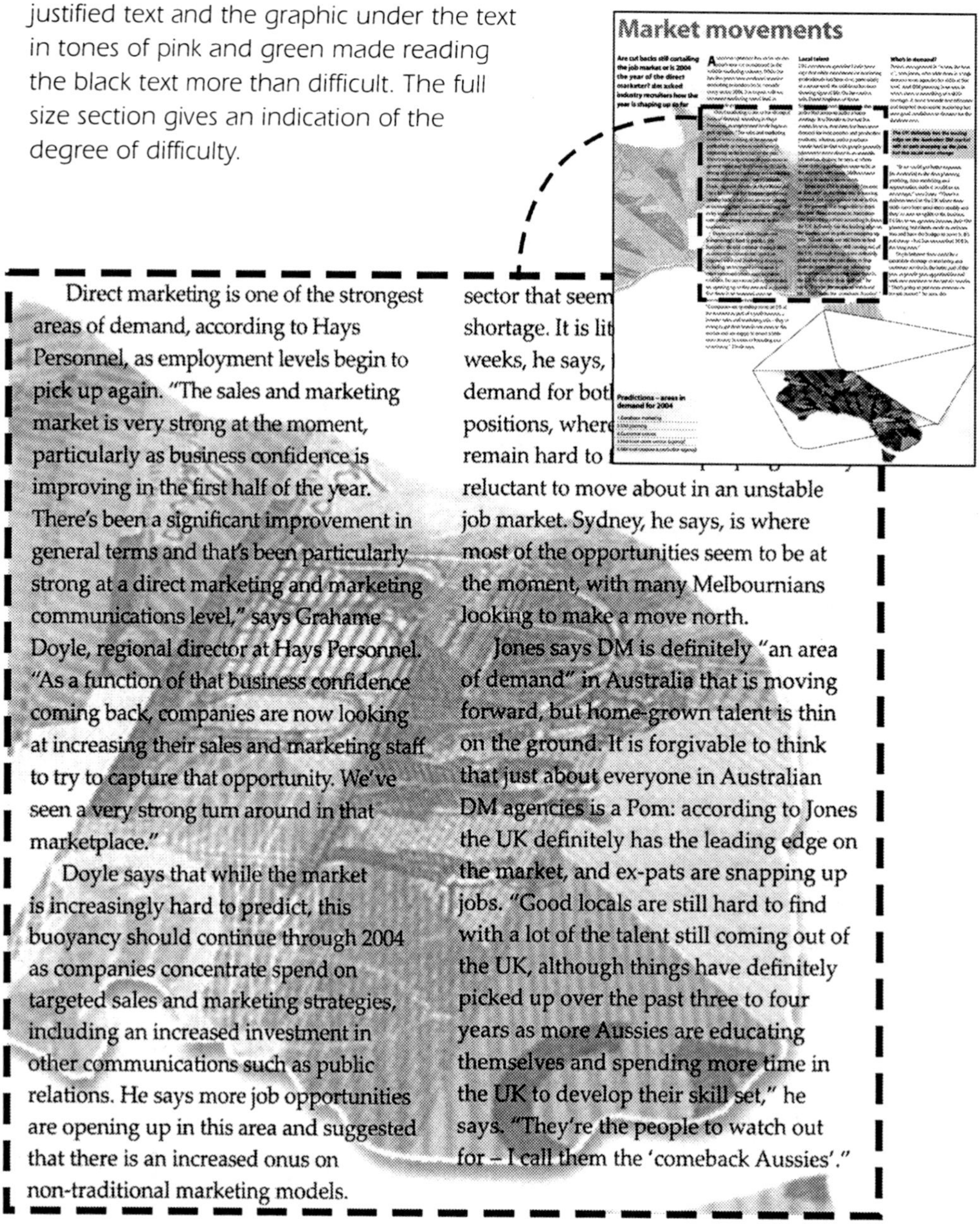

Direct marketing is one of the strongest areas of demand, according to Hays Personnel, as employment levels begin to pick up again. "The sales and marketing market is very strong at the moment, particularly as business confidence is improving in the first half of the year. There's been a significant improvement in general terms and that's been particularly strong at a direct marketing and marketing communications level," says Grahame Doyle, regional director at Hays Personnel. "As a function of that business confidence coming back, companies are now looking at increasing their sales and marketing staff to try to capture that opportunity. We've seen a very strong turn around in that marketplace."

Doyle says that while the market is increasingly hard to predict, this buoyancy should continue through 2004 as companies concentrate spend on targeted sales and marketing strategies, including an increased investment in other communications such as public relations. He says more job opportunities are opening up in this area and suggested that there is an increased onus on non-traditional marketing models.

sector that seem shortage. It is lit weeks, he says, demand for both positions, where remain hard to reluctant to move about in an unstable job market. Sydney, he says, is where most of the opportunities seem to be at the moment, with many Melbournians looking to make a move north.

Jones says DM is definitely "an area of demand" in Australia that is moving forward, but home-grown talent is thin on the ground. It is forgivable to think that just about everyone in Australian DM agencies is a Pom: according to Jones the UK definitely has the leading edge on the market, and ex-pats are snapping up jobs. "Good locals are still hard to find with a lot of the talent still coming out of the UK, although things have definitely picked up over the past three to four years as more Aussies are educating themselves and spending more time in the UK to develop their skill set," he says. "They're the people to watch out for – I call them the 'comeback Aussies'."

Not meant to be read!

Clearly, the spectacular graphic elements here were judged to be worth more than the words. So that's fine (but don't tell the writer).

FIGURE 85: A super amped designer doing an agile aerial! Compare this dynamic effect designed to convey a powerful message with the gratuitous violence to reading two pages back.

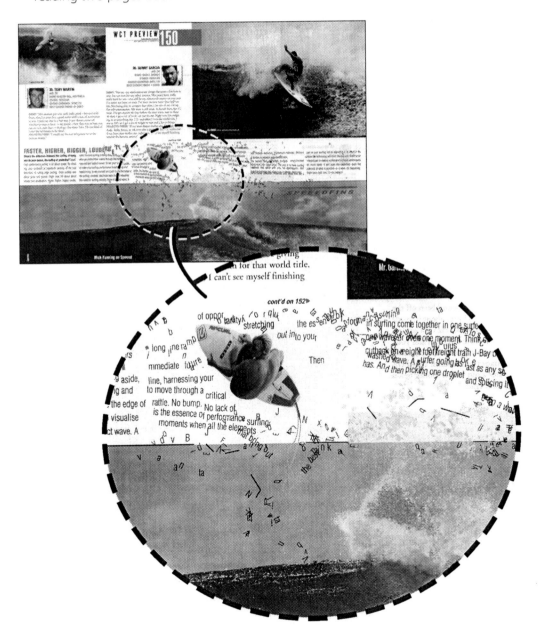

Lovely people, the Surfriders ...

The Surfriders Foundation brings together a lot of people around the world to do a lot of good work. With this classy looking full page ad. in *Surf International*, though, they are making it hard for anyone to join them by telling their story in a script face reversed out of black and no headline to provide an instant point of focus for the reader's eye.

FIGURE 86: Full page, glossy magazine advertisement.

86a (left): The original is marked by a terrific picture in tones of gold, but then the eye wanders until it locates the body text set in a script reversed out of black. Not good reading. The contact is even worse; the URL, www.surfrider.org, is printed in tiny size in bronze on black beneath the logo.

86b (right): The fix is basically adding a headline and setting the body in serif type, black on light gold. The face used here is Nofret, which in Regular is a pleasant serif style but in weightier italics leans towards calligraphy to provide a distinctive, but still readable headline. The signature is in SurfStyle script (what else?) as is the contact information.

Screamer headlines might not be read!

This local paper was delivered in thousands printed like this. How could they miss this screaming headline telling them to put a headline in place? It is set in 72 point Helvetica Condensed Black.

It is interesting to note that the experienced editor and proof reader, Gordon Woolf, the proprietor of The Worsley Press, who spotted this gaff did not see the headline error immediately either — rather, he spotted the *byline* error beneath it, set in lowly 10 point Helvetica Bold, *then*, once his eyes had been arrested, he noticed the headline error.

It raises an interesting question. Readers in the research cited here spoke of disliking "screaming" tabloid-style headlines in advertisements. Could it be that a 72 point headline like this one is just too big for comfortable reading on a tabloid page held at normal reading distance? This reader's eyes skated right over it, using it as a reading gravity signpost pointing him to where more comfortable reading began. An interesting research question. (Of course, the big headline on the front page does have a function, acting as a mini-poster on the newsstand.)

FIGURE 87: They pumped up the headline to screamer size … then didn't notice there was no headline in place! What does that say for screamer headlines?

Headline in h
and in here pl

By Byline1

PATIENTS are likely to get more satisfaction when they seek bulk-billed services from Dunkley electorate doctors next year.

The encouraging prospect is not dependent on

BRUCE BILLSON

DUNKLEY Federal Liberal MP Bruce Billson predicts his electorate's residents will benefit from "more affordable"

85 per cent the Medicar

"For a star surgery con:

Could granny read it in poor light?

Could granny read this page in poor light — or even at all? That's the question to ask about this children's choir program.

The page looks great, but as reading matter it suffers from half a dozen typographical and layout sins. In the end, one of its major failings is simple lack of consideration for the audience. This is the program for a children's choir. When children's choirs perform, there are lots of grandmothers and grandfathers in the audience and venues are often less than well lit. Combine the typographical nasties with the poor light and smeared granny glasses, and no reading can go on at all.

FIGURE 88: As a design, a piece of art to look at, this spread is delightul; dramatic, full of color and variation! But as a read …

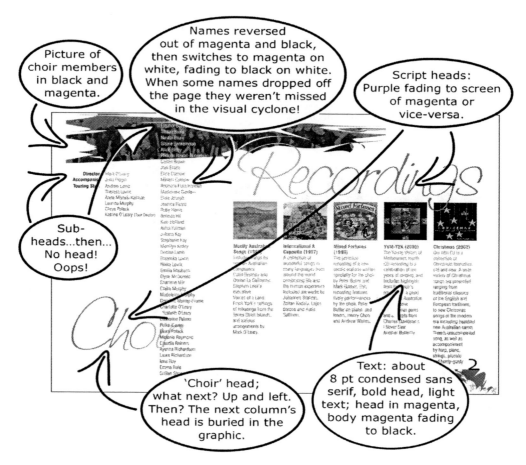

The Research Program

By Colin Wheildon

My father, a master printer in Derby, England, held three truths to be self-evident:

- Rules and borders must meet like water.
- Serif text is much easier to comprehend than sans serif text.
- Editors and designers are the missing link between the ape world and man.

The first tenet is inarguable.

That it took me a quarter of a century as an editor and designer before I questioned the validity of the second tenet is testimony, in some measure, to the truth of the third.

Early in my career I had become aware that the rules of typography were largely ancient maxims, with very little, if any, documented empirical evidence to support them.

I was aware of research into legibility, which is to say the intrinsic characteristics that make one type easier to read than another.

But I was also aware that research into mere legibility did not provide the answers I wanted.

The title of a newspaper set in Old English text may well be legible, but what would happen if the entire news and advertising content were to be set in Old English? Would it be comprehensible to anyone, other than perhaps a scholar of early English calligraphy or printing?

I had became a disciple of Edmund Arnold, formerly a professor of mass communications at Virginia Commonwealth University, Richmond VA.

FIGURE 89: It may be legible enough as a title, but extended use of Old English type would cause serious comprehension problems.

In a newspaper nameplate, Old English type like this is appropriate and expected. In the paper's news columns, it would take some getting used to.

Inspired by his common-sense teachings, but alarmed by the fact that even he depended on maxims rather than field research, I determined to subject some of those maxims to research.

This study is the result. It was conducted over a nine-year period, from 1982 to 1990.

The program examined several elements of typographic design. On two of them — the comprehensibility of serif type as opposed to sans serif in body matter, and the comprehensibility of lower case as opposed to capital letter headlines — there is, as I have indicated, some agreement, but very little observation of the agreement.

On three others — the use of color in headlines and in text, and the use of unjustified (ragged) setting, either left or right — there is either great disagreement or complete ignorance of the possible deleterious effects.

On a sixth element examined, whether italic body type is difficult or easy to comprehend, there appears to be a general, but ill-founded, agreement.

Texts on typography frequently allude to research into some of the elements to be examined, but, regrettably, discussion of this research is usually anecdotal rather than empirical.

In an attempt to test the reported findings of overseas research, the major part of this program was carried out in Sydney, Australia, in 1982-86.

About the participants

A total of 224 people, drawn from ten Sydney suburbs, completed the first program — a series of tests run over a period of five years.

The sample initially contained 300 people. As the years passed, some moved to other cities or towns, some died, some dropped out from sheer boredom, and some (I suspect) were committed to institutions for the chronically confused as a result of being bombarded at regular intervals with my experiment papers! All the results papers from those who dropped out were discarded and the responses from the 224 who completed all tests for that period were used for calculating the final results.

Initially, the sample had perfect balance of the sexes, comprising 150 men and 150 women. Fortunately and fortuitously, this balance was nearly maintained, the final figures being 113 men and 111 women.

There were no statistically significant differences between the responses from men and women.

At the beginning of the study, twenty of the readers were high school students. All the adults had completed four years of high school, and 178 (79 per cent) had reached matriculation level (high school graduation). Fifty-two (23 per cent) had acquired a university degree or professional or trade qualification, and 12 (five per cent) had acquired a higher degree. This represented a higher than average education level and obviously was a bias in the sample. This was deliberate. The participants were those who would be expected to take an interest in current events, and consequently would be likely to be regular newspaper and magazine readers.

In fact, all except two indicated they were consistent readers of a range of newspapers and other publications. The two exceptions, teenagers, said they read magazines regularly, but newspapers infrequently.

None of the readers was professionally involved in the printing or publishing industries. All were volunteers.

For the second series of tests, in 1986, the 224 subjects who had completed the first program were called upon again, augmented by a further 276 subjects to make a total of 500. The additional subjects were probably of generally similar background to the first group of subjects, although no attempt was made to identify their interests, education level or to classify them by socioeconomic background. Since this study was of short duration, there were no dropouts so the responses of all 500 subjects were incorporated into the final results.

The flyer study was carried out under the auspices of the National Roads and Motorists' Association (NRMA) in New South Wales beginning in 1988. The 224 original subjects from the first and second programs were again used for the initial comprehension tests. Thus alerted, the NRMA backed a major study conducted through its Public Relations and Research departments. The 15,000 participants were a random selection of members who were randomly assigned to subgroups as required for the different parts of the program. The 4,000 sub-sample used for the type sizes tests was randomly drawn from the 15,000.

Repeated measures

The question of repeated measurements of the same group of subjects has been raised by critics of my results.

Suffice to say that this procedure was approved by my academic and industry advisers who were very experienced in designing and carrying out valid research in the media and other disciplines.

As discussed below, the subjects were divided into two groups for most tests to provide for a control group or a contrasting group, the groups were switched from one parameter to the other, and over the period of five years, the subjects were returned to the total subject pool and reselected into test and control samples time and again.

A further consideration was that there was no logical connection between the different variables being tested. Variables like good reading gravity, type face and type style are all quite separate from each other so there is no need to change samples to measure their effects.

Finally, it ought to be noted that serif type, printed black on white, justified, with good reading gravity, was a variable or the control/baseline in test after test. Doubters should review the results for themselves — across all these tests involving different mixes of the subject pool and different texts, the findings for this combination remained rock solid.

Those with a different view are welcome to replicate my work!

The methodology

The methodology described is that which applied to the first program of the study (from 1982-85). Where it varied in the second and third programs, the difference has been noted (for example, the headline study was not based on comprehension, and that is noted and discussed in the text). That the flyer study went beyond type and layout is self-evident, but I felt readers interested in type and layout for both editorial and advertising publications would be interested in the other factors looked at.

To begin the program, I wrote two fictitious articles which were designed to have specific interest to members of the sample.

One article was about the plans for a local government authority to increase domestic rates, but to reduce the services. The article described the proposed changes in detail. This article was geographically specific to sample members and was aimed squarely at their pocketbooks.

The second article was about plans to place parking meters in suburban streets, particularly outside private houses, and to enforce on-street parking laws by constant police surveillance. It included police comments designed to inflame residents and to provoke reactions from them.

(Note that over the five years of the program, I wrote many articles about many subjects to use as test pieces; the two given here are simply examples.)

The subjects were divided into two equal groups to provide a measure of control. Each group read the same articles, but presented in alternative forms. Subjects were tested individually, in their own homes, under supervision, reading the material in a given time.

Initially, the articles were set in two design styles: one in the format of figure 10a (p.34), the other in the format of figure 10b (p.34). Half the subjects were given the Figure 10a layout, which complies with Arnold's Gutenberg Diagram. Half received the figure 10b layout, which does not.

Later, with another article, the sample groups were reversed. The first group was given the figure 10a layout, and the second group was given the figure 10b layout. This procedure was repeated several times over several years, and the sample groups were randomly selected each time from the subject pool each time. The same applied for the other reading gravity test, figure 12a and figure 12b (p.37) layouts.

For subsequent tests, serif versus sans serif, roman versus bold versus italic and so on, figure 10a became the standard layout. A few of these tests were also carried out using layout 10b too, but it was obvious that the reading gravity factor was confounding test outcomes, so it was dropped.

I conducted all the research. I devised the test pages, performed the interviews, phrased and asked the questions, and collated the results. I did it this way to eliminate the possibility of bias or distortion that might have occurred had I contracted others to do the work.

The final averages were taken from the total calculation, not as averages of a series of averages.

Assessment

The expectation was that participants who had fully read and comprehended the articles would be able to answer questions related to points throughout the them.

I had devised 10 questions about major points spread through each of the articles. When subjects had finished reading, these questions were asked in random order so as not to suggest any hierarchical relationship to the articles. My view was that if design or other factors had a detrimental effect on reading and comprehension, the point where comprehension declined would be apparent from incorrect answers.

For example, if subjects answered only two or three questions correctly, and these referred to points in the first few paragraphs of the article, it could be inferred that comprehension had failed after the first few paragraphs. If they answered seven or more questions correctly, then clearly they had read and understood the article. When the test results showed that one group had performed poorly, on average, compared with another group, and both were reading the same material which differed only by one element of typography or design, then it could be inferred that the change in that type or design element had had the effect of lowering or improving comprehension.

Those who correctly answered from 10 to seven questions were rated as having good comprehension; six to four, fair; and three to zero, poor.

Comments

Following each formal test, I asked informal questions in an attempt to gain introspective, anecdotal evidence. The answers to these questions helped to explain some of the results. For example, those reading text set in colored type generally performed poorly; from the informal questioning, I was able to find that participants experienced eye fatigue and consequent loss of comprehension. Colored headlines distracted readers from the black text which followed; discussion afterwards revealed how the distraction occurred.

What I told participants

Insofar as the artificial test situation allowed, I wanted the subjects to approach the reading tasks in a natural manner, as they might if they were casually reading a newspaper or magazine, so I was careful not to spell out what I was trying to elucidate, nor to mislead them in a particular direction, either of which might have resulted in biased test results.

Rather, I indicated that the tests were designed to help me, as a magazine editor (the NRMA's members' magazine, *Open Road*), to produce better material for my readers. I believe some of them assumed the improvement was to be in the content rather than the presentation, and I did not disabuse them.

My advisors

The catalyst for the methodology and procedures I used was the late Professor Henry Mayer, Professor of Political Science at Sydney University, NSW, Australia, and editor of the learned magazine *Media Information Australia*. When I mentioned to him that I was considering some research into elements of design and typography, he gave me several invaluable pieces of advice.

Professor Mayer's first piece of advice was to produce an acceptable methodology. There would be critics, he said, mainly among those who found the results disturbed their comfortable beds of subjective prejudice. They would attack on two fronts: ad hominem, which could be countered with ease, and on the method. If the method were faulty, the attack could not be countered.

Moreover, he said, if he found the methodology faulty he would personally crucify me, irrespective of whether the results confirmed or opposed his own prejudices about design.

The next piece of advice was that I should attempt to eliminate all variables when testing a particular element. This advice led to a long sequence of experiments in which questionable design elements were progressively eliminated.

Professor Mayer also advised me to circulate the proposed methodology and results widely before publishing. If possible, he said, present them personally to a public forum, preferably to potential critics. This I did, using the Australian Creative Advertising Awards (the Caxtons), and the Australian Suburban Newspapers Association Congress, as forums.

I then sought the advice of Professor Edmund Arnold, then Professor of Mass Communications at Virginia Commonwealth University, Richmond, VA, USA, and Professor Rolf Rehe, then of the Purdue Universities Consortium in Indianapolis, IN, USA. Assisted by Professor Mayer, I adapted Rolf Rehe's rate-of-work method to suit my experiments.

Professor Mayer also advised me on sample selection.

I was advised on the conduct of the project by Dr Simon Gadir, then Director of Research for the Newspaper Advertising Bureau of Australia. Dr. Gadir also advised me on such factors as statistical significance of results, and scales of confidence (the McLemar scale) — in other words, which numbers would stand up to scientific scrutiny, and which should be (and were) eliminated.

I also sought advice on method, calculation, analysis, and presentation of results from the following:

- Professor David Sless, Executive Director of the Communications Research Institute of Australia.
- Professors Arnold, Rehe, and Mayer.
- David Ogilvy, who was a renowned researcher before he became the

doyen of modern advertising.

- Bryce Courtenay, who when he is not writing bestselling novels and screenplays (*The Power of One*), was Creative Director for the George Patterson Advertising Agency in Sydney.
- Members of the academic staff of the University of Reading, UK, which houses the British Government's forms design center.
- Members of the academic staff of the Royal College of Arts in London.
- Jim Thomson, then Head of Research for the National Roads and Motorists' Association (NRMA), Australia, one of the ten biggest motoring organizations in the world.

Comprehension or readability?

Over the years of my research, David Ogilvy more than once raised the question whether I was measuring reading comprehension or merely readability. I'm grateful for his persistence in moving me to confront this important and difficult question.

My difficulty stemmed from the fact that, in my *Shorter Oxford Dictionary*, readability has two distinct definitions:

1. Capable of being read, legible.
2. Capable of being read with pleasure or interest, usually of a literary work.

This presented me with a dilemma. I was not testing legibility; that is a totally different discipline and has been the subject of a considerable measure of scientific work. I wanted to know whether the nature of type or design affected the reader's ability to *understand* the text.

However, if I used the words readability and readable, they could be misconstrued as being analogous to legibility and legible.

So I settled on comprehensibility.

The essence is, as David Ogilvy suggests, that I was measuring the extent to which typography and design affected understanding. But to understand, one first has to read the message

However, in Chapter 6, where I address the subject of headlines, I did not test comprehension, because the method did not permit it. There, I was testing whether headlines were easy to read or not. Those were the words used in the tests, and those were the words used by the sample participants.

On color, type, reading and the eyes

By Geoffrey Heard

The test outcomes which show that almost any departure from the standard of black serif type on white (or light) paper results in some interference to the reader's ability to read and comprehend text, are consistent with the results of psychological experimentation in these and related fields.

Certainly, when I first read Colin Wheildon's book, it gave rise to a number of "Aha!" moments in my mind. My studies in psychology included vision, information acquisition, reading and information processing in the brain. "Aha!", I cried, the moment I saw Colin Wheildon's results on the use of high chroma colors in headlines, then "Aha!" I cried again when I read the results of reading non-black/dark body type and color on color, and yet again "Aha!" when I read the outcomes of his tests on type set justified, ragged left and ragged right.

Color

The fact that high chroma colored headlines keep intruding into reading of the body type under them fitted perfectly with the notion of the primacy of color, hard-wired into very low levels of the human brain, over the learned skill of reading. Psychologists have speculated that just such colors have been the signs of danger for humankind reaching far back down the evolutionary chain, so when we see them they absolutely demand attention. Certainly, recognition of such colors is wired into very low levels of the human brain — and for good reason. Think of the nocturnal animal from which we evolved, scuttling around in the jungle. In that environment, red and other high chroma colors often are the signs of danger — toxic plants and venomous animals. Back in World War II, Australian and American personnel on active service in the Southwest Pacific theatre were issued with a little booklet to help them live off the land if they were forced to do so. Called *Friendly Fruits & Vegetables*, it carried this dire warning on page 3: "In general, red means danger in the jungle, so that unknown red fruits and berries should be avoided." So now you know! If our little ancestor hadn't learned this, we might not be here!

Psychologists demonstrate the power of this primacy of the hard-wired versus the learned skill of reading by running a simple experiment with a tachistoscope — a tube with subject matter at one end which is illuminated by a flash of light of variable duration, while the observer looks into the other end, allowing no light to enter from there. When a card with the word "green" printed in red ink is exhibited, the observer has no difficulty in reading it when lit by longer flashes. However, when the flash duration shortens into the $^1/_{30}$th-$^1/_{60}$th of a second level, the color takes over from the written form. The observer knows s/he has seen a word, but the understanding of the word is driven by the color of it. "Green" is what is written, but the observer confidently reports the color of the type, insisting that they have read the word "red"! Duller colors are less effective in taking over from the word and letter shapes.

How we see

It would be reasonable to suggest that the physiology of the human eye and the way we read come into play too in the way attention — and the focus of the eyes — is dragged away from the text by the bright headline and the difficulty experienced in reading non-black body text and color on color.

In seeing generally, including reading, our eyes are constantly on the move. Comparing our vision with a camera, we have a very wide angle view — we see right out to the sides — but the definition of 95% of the field is rotten. Only the fovea, the central part of the retina, the light sensitive cells in the back of our eyes, is both in focus and packed with color receptors. Further out, in the parafovea, receptors are further apart and sense light and dark only — very good at allowing us to detect movement but no good for detail. We compensate for this by keeping our eyes constantly on the move, we pick out something vaguely seen in the periphery, then move our eyes to bring it into sharp focus and full definition and color.

Even as I was writing this, I detected a movement, a small, dark shape apparently moving along the top of the fence outside my window. What was it? A bird, a cat, something else? My eyes *immediately and involuntarily* flicked around enough to identify the shape and color as the top of my neighbor's red cap as he cycled down his drive.

The investigation of attention, vision, reading and a whole raft of other activities has greatly benefited from the use of the technique of filming and more recently, video recording, eye movements, like that done by Professor Vogele (see figure 68, p.104). The recording is made while a person is reading or looking at an object, the eye movements are mapped, then the map is overlaid on the target document or field. Among other things, this technique has shown that by far the most attractive thing to the human eye is other human eyes and human faces generally. (It's no surprise when you think about it; children are born with their eyes prefocused for the distance from their mother's breast to her face.) That makes the picture of a human face an excellent illustration to put in that fallow top right-hand corner of your page, incidentally adjoining Arnold's Primary Optical Area. Put it at the Terminal Anchor point, bottom right-hand corner, and you can kiss your reader good-bye! They will flick their eyes to the face, and be inclined to slide right off to the next page!

How we read

We start reading by learning to recognize the shape of single letters and attaching them to sounds. Then we move up to working on combinations of two letters into the very simplest words (he, it), then three letter, four letter, and longer words. As we read more and more, we

FIGURE 90: Eye movements during fluent reading. The stars mark fixation points, the dotted lines the saccades or jumps. A less fluent reader might jump from word to word or even letter to letter. The fluent reader, expecting 'fox', fixates on 'rhinoceros' then does a double take just to be sure!

learn to recognize whole words at a glance (whether by the shape of the word or by recognizing individual letters still and processing them at lightning speed is still being debated by researchers). Some people stop right there, but most move on to become skilled, mature or fluent readers — recognizing combinations of words as phrases and more. As our language skills develop, we also learn what words go together so that when we are reading our minds summon up the short list of expected words or phrases that the construction of the text, the vocabulary being used, subject matter, context and so on suggest could possibly fit. As we read on and gather more and more information, we automatically shorten this menu.

The eye camera shows our eyes move in fits and starts. Our eyes fixate on a point, dwell for a moment, then leap in a smooth saccade further down the line to the next salient point. In reality, we are reading several words ahead of where we are consciously looking and if the word or words out ahead match what we expect to see, we may not even "read" them; we will take them "as read" and our next saccade will jump to a point beyond to scan the next bunch of words. Conversely, if we notice an unfamiliar, unusual or unexpected word coming up (like 'rhinoceros' instead of 'fox' in figure 90 (p.143), for example, we definitely will fixate on that and make an extra long stop there, then even check back again just to make sure that what we read was correct. And all this happens quite unconsciously!

At the end the line, we jump back to the beginning of the next line in one long, smooth saccade, apparently using our knowledge of where the left hand edge of the text is (Arnold's Axis of Orientation) and the white space between lines for guidance plus our expectation of what the first word(s) of the new line will be, to make an accurate leap across and down. Notice how you can "lose your place" if the line spacing (leading or interlinear spacing) is not adequate — or if it is excessive. Our reliance on the left hand edge of the block or column of type (Vogele's Axis of Orientation) helps explain why type set ragged left is so difficult to read.

Something else we ought to note is that most people are very good at picking up patterns and that we unconsciously and consciously use them. Thus we have fully justified type, so that both the line beginnings and the line endings start on the same measure on the page (like this book) and before we have read more than a couple of lines, our eyes are using the known beginning and ending point as guides. No searching fruitlessly for more words out in the great white paper desert beyond the end of lines; the eyes jump back a known distance without looking further. The change involved in short lines at the end of paragraphs and indents at the beginning indicate a change in circumstances to us — which is why such small changes work so well as paragraph markers.

If type is "set left", that is, ragged right so that line endings vary, there is the loss of the patterned cue for eye movement and the jump back to the left is different with each line. The research cited in this book shows

FIGURE 91: Scientists believe our eyes see something like this at each fixation.

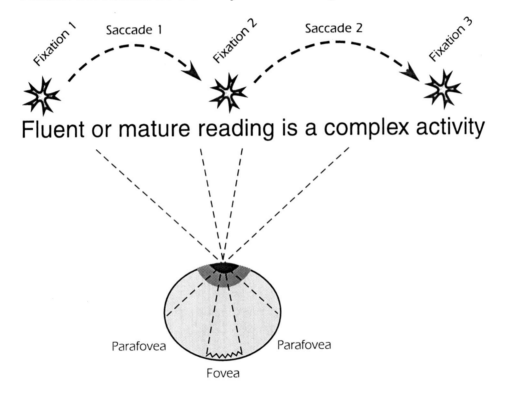

that this interferes somewhat with our ability to read and comprehend text. When copy is set left and ragged right, the saving grace is that we do know *where* on the page to jump to (the Axis of Orientation). If type is set right, that is, ragged left, so that line beginnings vary, it might be theorized that the jump back is a leap into the unknown, making reading harder. Colin Wheildon's research bears out that hypothesis.

Word shape versus letter shape

There is argument among reading psychologists about the extent to which the accomplished reader uses and processes individual letters while reading. The individual letters school argues that with practise, people can read type in any face set at sharp angles, upside down, inverted left-right, or all capitals just as fast as they read conventionally set type.

On the face of it, this appears to be at odds with Colin Wheildon's research results. But it is not — Colin Wheildon is telling us what type and layout makes it *easiest* for most people to read and comprehend text now, today, not what a few individuals can do after intensive training.

The willingness to read and thus to understand, is what comes into play here. **As noted elsewhere, official Germany used Fette Fraktur extensively as a body type.** But although everyone could read it at a good clip, messages were not getting out. Did people *choose* not to read because it was too much like hard work? The change was made to Helvetica and communication improved. (There is a move to revive a modern Fraktur. Its proponents claim great readability, but research seems to be lacking.)

Our aim as communications professionals constructing advertisements, brochures, letters, flyers, magazines, newsletters, or newspapers, is to win the interest of the maximum number of readers, have the maximum number of them read and comprehend what we have written, and thus sell them our product or convey our ideas to them. Colin Wheildon's research provides us with information about what type and layout best does that. We ought to take note of his results. If we want to run a campaign to change reading preferences, we rather than convey a message now, today, then we ought to advise our clients or employers of that fact ... and prepare to find employment elsewhere.

Conclusions

All of this explains several things:
* How a high chroma color headline captures our attention and interferes with reading. Our eyes bounce along the line of type, come to the end and ... search for the beginning of the next line. But there is a glimpse

of the color in the headline, the primary response takes over, and our focus is back up on the headline before we know it instead of moving down to continue reading on the next line. Think of those people doing Colin Wheildon's reading test who folded the page so the colored headlined was out of sight. They knew what was happening!

- If color interferes like this, how it is that a light screen of high chroma color under black text can act as an eye magnet *and* allow good reading? It is simple — when reading, the eyes are being cued by the brain to seek type. High chroma color type can grab the eyes because of its intensity and because it also meets the criterion the eyes are searching on — type! A light tint of high chroma color behind black type is not only less intense, but it is not type shaped. But in general terms, that high chroma background *must* be light and the item *must* be short or we start to lose reader comprehension because reading *is* a bit harder. And we have seen how rapidly comprehension deteriorates as the color screen gets stronger.

- How decorated or otherwise unusual fonts interfere with our reading. Think about this: someone is writing about a drunk. We read: "There, in the middle of the footpath staring reproachfully at him, stood a big, pink … " Hands up everyone who did *not* know that the next word was going to be "elephant"? But even when we are so sure, if that sentence or even just that word were written in a different, decorative font, we would be forced to read it, perhaps even spell it out: instead of elephant, we might have elevator or eggplant, or even 'elephone. It would not look right.

- Why setting blocks of text ragged right and ragged left interfere with reading and comprehension (see discussion p.144).

Given what we know about how people see and how skilled or mature readers read, Colin Wheildon's results simply make sense, don't they?

FIGURE 92: This graphic combines several aspects of the easy-to-understand material prepared by researcher, Aries Arditi, PhD, for the Lighthouse International website, http://www.lighthouse.org. These graphics derive from those Dr Arditi uses in support of a discussion on the use and abuse of color; presented on the website in full color But even rendered into grayscale as here, they are still valuable, dramatising the loss of contrast between colors experienced by those with color vision disability and those whose sight is deteriorating.

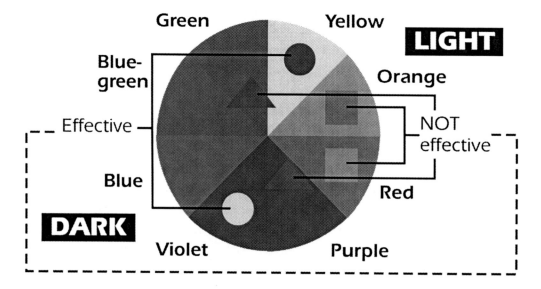

92a: Violet on yellow and yellow on violet (a reverse) work well, but red on orange and vice versa and green on purple and vice versa do not work well even when there is some contrast in the colors. In general, mix the light and dark colors, not dark and dark or light and light. A color on a shade of itself is definitely a 'no-no'.

92b: Dark blue on light yellow crosses the dark/light line and works well; mising adjacent colors from above the line, orange on yellow, is not effective.

By Geoffrey Heard

Colin Wheildon's research covers the majority of the population who can be described as fluent readers — they have achieved adult reading capabilities so that they can read and understand scores or even hundreds of words a minute.

It is estimated that in nations like the USA, United Kingdom, Canada, Australia and New Zealand, western industrialized nations with universal education, that group comprises between 80 and 90 per cent of the population aged upwards from mid-teens.

But what of the 10 to 20 per cent of the population who are not fluent readers and others who may have some kind of vision impairment, such as a form of color blindness, which does not impinge on their ability to read ordinary text but may have relevance where particular combinations of colors are used?

The gathering and presentation of statistics varies, but it would appear that our populations include:

- One to three per cent of people who have a vision impairment serious enough to impinge on reading ability.
- A similar proportion of people who have a physical impairment other than vision which interferes with reading (such as the inability to hold a book steady).
- Something of the order of 10 per cent of the population who cannot or have not learned to read or have achieved only a low level of reading. They include people who were once fluent readers but who can no longer read with their former fluency because of illness, accident, or the impact of aging on their eyes or other relevant physical functions.

Research has shown that all these people do not read in standard ways and has also highlighted the fact that they cannot be categorized simply. However, while their reading abilities cover a wide range, responding to them is relatively straightforward since, except for extreme cases where people need specific vision enhancement technologies, for example, best practice in type and layout is similar for many different cases because while the causes of their difficulties in reading are different, they result in similar reading processes. They are, in effect, immature readers, blocked for one reason or another from moving to a higher level or forced down from the higher level by acquired physical or mental impairment.

Reading mode

As discussed earlier, the fluent or mature reader's eyes bounce along a line of text, covering a span of perhaps a dozen characters. Research clearly shows that the reader is matching what she or he sees against an expectation of what should be there which is constantly changing as the reader assimilates more and more information from the page. In the end, this rolling process results in what we know as "reading" — we translate the marks on the page into language, an essentially verbal thing.

Clearly, someone with a vision impairment cannot read in this manner. If their vision is blurry, even with glasses or contact lenses, they need bigger letters to see more easily, they need simpler shapes, they need higher contrast — it helps if edges are emphasized, they need no confusion about shapes, and so on. Someone with a narrowed field of vision simply cannot scan the ordinary length lines in the two or three leaps of the person with unimpaired vision — they must make smaller jumps. Both these people can use extra space between lines simply to make it easier to focus on the line they are reading and extra space between letters, but not too much, to keep distracting shapes out of their limited vision.

The same applies for many people who do not read well due to poor learning early in life or a specific learning disability. In most cases, they do better with larger and simpler type, more space between lines, etc. which helps them to more easily focus on and recognize letters and words.

Type and layout solutions

The type and layout guidelines given below for those who are not optimal/fluent/mature readers which are given here in no way pretend to be a manual on how to set type and lay out publications for the vision or reading impaired. Rather, the intention is to introduce the field to typesetters, designers and desktop publishers, to all users of type, and to pass on a notion of what the solutions are and where more detailed information may be gathered.

While we are talking here about a different class of readers from those covered by Colin Wheildon's research, it is also worth noting that many of the recommendations for the vision or reading impaired, such as providing type with the best contrast, hold good for all readers. There are notable differences, however.

The primary differences are:

- Type size — suggested type sizes for the Clear Print category (see below) start at 12 point, the middle of the range fluent readers prefer (see Table 21, p.111), or 14 point, the very top of that range. Starting type sizes for Large Print (see below) are 16-18 points.
- Type face — sans serif faces are preferred with the alternative being the simpler serif faces, the opposite of Colin Wheildon's research outcomes for fluent readers. Faces that are large for their nominal point size and have large 'x' height are preferred.
- Spacing — non-fluent readers want more space around their letters. This makes sense if they are literally reading letter by letter; they don't want letters crowding together and distracting them.
  - — Leading: fluent readers prefer ten to fifteen per cent leading. Large Print readers want about twice as much.
  - — Type spacing: Monospaced faces help Large Print readers by ensuring that narrow letters, like 'i', are not crowded by their neighbors as they may be in proportionally spaced type.
- Setting — Set left, ragged right, is universally agreed to be best versus fluent readers' preference for fully justified, clearly reflecting the different reading modes.

FIGURE 93: *Clear Print and Large Print preferred type faces and sizes*

For Clear Print, Helvetica 12 point or better, 14 point, is a good choice; Bookman is one of the better serif choices in 12 point or 14 point, not forgetting extra leading.

For Large Print, either of the above works, but this example is Geneva in 18/24 point size for 30 per cent (6 point) leading. Monospaced type, like Andale Mono, might be even better.

Information was drawn from four primary sources: The Lighthouse International organization and the American Printing House (APH) for the Blind in the USA, the Royal Institute for the Blind (RNIB) in the UK, and the Roundtable on Reading Material for People with Print Disabilities Inc. for Australia and New Zealand. Their guidelines for action are very similar. They are based on a mix of research, stated reader preference and experience.

All sources specifically noted that research is ongoing.

Clear Print

The RNIB has a category the others do not have — Clear Print — which is intended for those with relatively limited vision impairment and thus limited difficulty in reading.

The guidelines it lays out are generally similar to those it and other organizations provide for large print work, but less marked. The big difference is in type size. The RNIB's Clear Print solution calls for type which is a minimum of 12 point size and preferably 14 point, while type sizes of 16-18 points and up are advocated for Large Print.

Large Print

The figure below brings together in tabular form recommendations of all four major sources used.

Figure 94: Large print recommendations from four organizations.

Lighthouse	APH	RNIB	Roundtable
1. Body text type should be 16-18 points and upwards			
16-18 pts	18 pts; 9 pt x-height	16-18 pts	14-18 pts
2. Heads and sub-heads			
—	Bigger & bolder	Ditto	Ditto
3. Type face			
Sans may be better	Sans serif Have own face	Sans or serif	Sans, e.g. Arial Univers, Helvetica
4. Type style			
Roman, regular, upper & lower case	Ditto	Avoid italics, condensed, extended use of capitals	Ditto. Use bold for emphasis

5. Type color			
Black on white is best for contrast	Ditto	Ditto	Ditto, black on buff for some
6. Reversed			
White or yellow out of black best for some	—	Ensure field is dark	—
7. Letter Spacing			
Monospaced is best	Ditto	Ditto	Ditto
8. Word spacing			
Fixed	Ditto	Ditto	Ditto
9. Leading/Line spacing			
At least 25-30% of type size	Ditto	Ditto	Ditto, but don't overdo it
10. Alignment			
—	Set left (ragged right) to avoid varied spacing	Do not run text around graphics	Ditto
11. Line length			
—	—	60-70 letters for Clear Print, less for Large Print	—
12. Paper			
Matt	Matt	Matt and heavier than average	Ditto

Comments

In addition to the above, each of the authorities had some specific comments which are worth noting.

Lighthouse goes into some detail about the use of high color contrasts, and on their site, have some actual examples. Some elements of them have been reproduced here (p. 148) in grayscale to portray the flavor of them. In some respects, grayscale presentation is an advantage for normally sighted readers who are preparing to use color in this field as it demonstrates how drastically contrast is reduced when color is removed or saturation lost, as is the case for those with color blindness or loss of visual sensitivity.

APH notes that graphics from each end of the color spectrum — full color or black line drawings — are best to ensure contrast; grayscale graphics are to be avoided. Graphics should not interfere with type and vice versa. Care needs to be taken to ensure that such graphics as maps and diagrams follow the text guidelines. Graphics needs to be sized up just as type does.

RNIB notes the need to keep text horizontal (obviously they are talking about English and similar languages), make layout simple, have large gutters between columns where columns are used, to ensure navigational aids such as page headings and numbers are kept in the same place on the page, and that if a printed document is to be folded, the fold does not interfere with the type.

Roundtable notes that while black printed on white (or vice versa) makes for the strongest contrast, there is a case for using paper which is off-white to light yellow. While this reduces contrast slightly, many readers report it provides a pleasant reading experience, and a number of authorities on dyslexia note that the highest possible contrast produced by black and white actually impedes some people with dyslexia learning to read.

Since the various organizations active in all these fields emphasize that research is ongoing, the guidelines each produces are subject to change as new knowledge is gained.

Those wishing to produce materials in this field should check with the organizations for the latest version of their full guidelines.

Some references in this field

- http://www.lighthouse.org/print_leg.htm
  Making Text Legible
  Designing for People with Partial Sight
  by Aries Arditi, Ph.D
- http://www.aph.org/edresearch/lpguide.htm
  APH Educational Research
  Large Print: Guidelines for Optimal Readability and APHont™
    a font for low vision
- http://www.rnib.org.uk/xpedio/groups/public/documents/
  PublicWebsite/public_seeitright.hcsp
  RNIB See It Right Pack.

There is no better way to get a handle on the language of type and layout than to see where it all came from. A handful of decades ago, you probably could have achieved that by calling in at your local print shop — many printers had an old press, old typesetting equipment and examples of old type gathering dust at the back of the shop. Some kept an old flatbed press and some handset type on hand for that occasional special job which would never look right printed on more modern equipment.

These days, though, most of the old print shops or typesetting shops have gone and so have the people who worked in them and knew what the old equipment was all about. There are a small number of traditional printers still around handling special jobs, but in the general commercial world, the desktop computer with an integrated type and layout program — desktop publishing, DTP — has swept all before it. So a trip down the typesetting and printing industry's memory lane means a visit to a print museum.

The language of typography mostly comes from the days of handset metal type. Each character was cast in mirror image on a block of metal. The blocks — all of the same size for that font — were fitted into a frame to produce the whole page in mirror reverse. Where necessary, spacers were added to fill blank space, make word spaces, spread out the type along the lines and to add space between the lines.

Once all the type and any other material, such as lines, nice fancy bits to embellish the page and so on were in place, the type was locked down with wedges, an ink pad was run over it to ink the type and a sheet of paper was pressed down on it (hence "the press") to transfer the inked image to the paper, then it was lifted off. Voila! The page was printed! We mimic the process with woodcuts, potato cuts and so on.

A system of measurements grew up around type which continues to be used today.

Type

Individual letters, figures or punctuation marks are called characters. A *face* or *type face* is a particular type, for example, Times, Helvetica, Garamond or Univers. The large letters are *capitals* (*caps* for short) or upper case characters; the small letters are *lower case*. They are called upper case or lower case because typesetters used to have their loose type ready to hand in two boxes or cases; the capitals were in the upper case and the small letters in the lower case. A *style* is the form of characters, e.g. roman, regular, italic, bold, extended, condensed, etc. A *font* is a complete alphabet of one face and one style in both upper case and lower case letters, with figures and punctuation marks. We have a *type family* if we group together all the type sizes and styles of a particular type face.

FIGURE 95: This is a type family of the Caslon face made up of two fonts — book and italic.

FIGURE 96: A display cap letter for hand-set type.

abcdefghijklmnopqrstuvwxyz
ABCDEFGHIJKLMNOPQRSTUVWXYZ
1234567890-=[]\;',./
1@#$%^&*()_+{}|:"<>?

abcdefghijklmnopqrstuvwxyz
ABCDEFGHIJKLMNOPQRSTUVWXYZ
1234567890-=[]\;',./
1@#$%^&()_+{}|:"<>?*

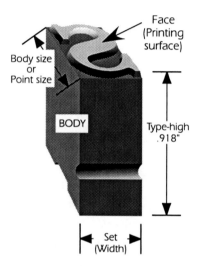

Face (Printing surface)

Body size or Point size

BODY

Type-high .918"

Set (Width)

Measures

The basic unit of measurement of type is the *point*. There were 72.26 points to the inch in days gone by; in the computer age (thank goodness) this has been changed to exactly 72 points to the inch (2.54 cm). The next measure is picas; with 12 points to the pica and 6 picas to the inch. Type size is measured exclusively in points; line lengths used to be measured in picas and still may be, but this measurement is falling into disuse in many places, particularly those where metric measurement is used. In former times, the pica was important because it was vital that line lengths be an exact number of points — it made setting with metal type, with its limited range of spacing devices, much easier. With computerized systems, virtually infinite variability of spacing is possible so having an exact point width for columns or blocks of type is less important.

Type size, point size, or *body size* was the vertical measurement of the

face of the block of metal — the body — on which the character sat. If the type size was 12 point, this block was 12 points high. The characters themselves might be all or nearly all of that 12 points high, but they might be only 8 or 9 points high — but because they sat on that 12 point body, they were called 12 point type. Type continues to be specified by point height, and difference faces continue to vary significantly from that nominal measure.

The width of the blocks on which the characters sat varied with the widths of the characters. 'M' or 'W' is the widest and '/' the narrowest in metal type. This width is the *natural* setting. While 'M' would fill the whole width of the block it sat on, narrow letters like 'i' might have three or four points each side of it so it would not appear crushed by its neighboring letters. The period or full-stop '.' sat on about a half em (we'll come to that in a moment) wide block which, along with a full em space, gave special emphasis to the space between sentences. Computer type setting systems retain the extra space around the narrow letters, but most have dropped the extra space for the period.

Most computer systems follow the old convention of type families in providing a predefined range from 5 to 72 points in size. In fact, of course, computerized type can be much smaller or much bigger than that and can vary infinitely in between — although usually restricted to quarter or half point increments by programmers.

Not to be confused with the *type size*, for example 12 point or 36 point, which is the height of the type, is an old measure called *type-high*. This is the depth of the block the character sat on; obviously it needed to be a standard measurement so that the typesetter would get a flat page.

The point

The story of the point measure is worth telling because it is so odd. Way back when, printers made their own type any

---

FIGURE 97: *The points rule used to rule the printers' shop. Printed full size … but beware, the page might have shrunk!*

size they liked. In 1737, Pierre Simon Fournier, in France, proposed a standardized system of 72 points to the inch. Printers were eager to adopt it but unfortunately, the paper on which Fournier printed and distributed his scales shrank inconsistently, so everyone was close but not identical! Thirty-three years later, his countryman, François Didot, proposed a standard of 72 points to the French inch and it was quickly adopted in France and around Europe.

The French inch is 1.0638 English and US inches which might have been one of the reasons (along with the Napoleonic wars) Didot's system did not succeed in the UK and US as well as it might have done. As it was, the English-speaking world did not have a standardized system for another 101 years, until the Marder, Luse & Co. type foundry lost everything in the Great Chicago Fire and set about redesigning from scratch. Nelson Hawks did the job, taking his measure from a popular pica size at the time, and determining the point to be 0.013838 of a UK and US inch — resulting in yet another bastard measure, since 72 points equalled 0.996336 of an inch. Despite that problem, it was adopted widely.

When Warnock and Geschke created PostScript in the 1980s (see p.160), they plumped for stretching the point (pun intended!) a smidgen to make it exactly $\frac{1}{72}$ of an inch over an underlying measurement of $\frac{1}{1440}$ of an inch (called a twip). Old timers huffed and puffed, but the fact was that Warnock and Geschke were actually implementing a system which was older than the old timers' system. The Postscript (or Fournier) point is now the standard worldwide.

Spacing

Word spacing was achieved by using *em quads* or parts of them. An *em quad* was a little block of metal which measured the same as the type size in both height and width. Another way of specifying an *em* was to make it equal to the width of the lower case 'm' in the font. An *en* was (and is!) the same but half the width of an *em*. Then there were 3-to-the-em, 4-to-the-em and 5-to-the-em spacers; their names speak for themselves. Normal or natural word spacing is a third of an em. In our computerized systems, we use the *em* and the *en* — think of the em-dash and the en-dash (but also think how variable they are from font to font) — but the finer spacings have gone; we can now do them to the exact measure *we* want in our computers.

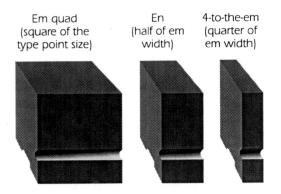

Em quad
(square of the
type point size)

En
(half of em
width)

4-to-the-em
(quarter of
em width)

FIGURE 98: Em, en and
4-to-the-em spacers in metal
type for handsetting.

Letter spacing could be varied above *natural* in metal type days by slipping 1 point brass spacers between characters. There were also ½ point and even ¼ point available — or for a very thin space, paper! That was simple enough, but it was the devil to remove space — lead had to be sawn, planed or ground off the side of the character blocks which might leave them either useless at worst or a nuisance at best for future work which did not need the reduced interletter spacing. On computer systems, we happily play with *loose tracking/letter loosening* and *tight tracking/letter tightening/automatic kerning*; it is just a matter of selecting the type and clicking a command. Likewise, *kerning* between pairs of letters, particularly useful in display sizes between such pairs as Fa, Ta, Te, Tr, OX, and so on, is simplicity itself.

We can safely disregard the *unit* measurement system. It varied wildly from type foundry to type foundry and from size to size. In essence, the width of the *em* was divided into so many units, ranging from 4 to 64 (although many used 18). The width of the unit, in points, varied according to the size of the type, so this introduced a proportional measurement. We don't have to worry about this today because it is built into our computer systems. We are actually using a 100 unit measure when we set our automatic or manual *kerning* to .01, .25 or whatever. Since this is a decimal-based system, it is the same as percentages so it does not need special consideration.

Line spacing is *leading* (pronounced *ledding*, as in the amount of lead metal). Where no extra space is added between lines, the type is *set solid*. Commonly a little extra space was added between lines of type by inserting strips of lead, varying from 1 point up. 1, 2, 3 and 4 point wide strips were called *leads* and thicker strips, 6 points and up, were called *slugs*. A setting would specify the *size, leading, face* and *style*. A setting might be 11/13 Goudy Roman or a head might be 24/26 Helvetica Bold. The first figure is the *size* in points and the second the height of the line in points, comprising the specified height of the type and the added leading.

PostScript®

In typesetting and desktop publishing, this is the computer language used to describe pages and their contents for the output device such as a laser printer or imagesetter. It is also used to draw screen images. Increasingly, it is being replaced by PDF, Portable Document Format, which is a compacted form of PostScript. Both technologies are owned by Adobe Systems Inc. and are widely licensed and emulated. John Warnock developed PostScript's precursor, Interpress, while working for Xerox at its famous Parc research facility. When Xerox decided not to take the product to market, Warnock and his then boss, Charles Geschke, decided to do it themselves. They founded Adobe Inc., developed and refined PostScript v.1, then linked with Apple Computer which was going into the market with the first Macintosh (relying on a graphical interface also with roots in Parc), and the desktop publishing revolution was born. Warnock and Geschke had thought of building their own printer, but instead stuck with software, licensing PostScript to computer and printer makers everywhere so that it rapidly became a standard.

Some more information

Microsoft tongue in cheek — yet factual

Microsoft presents excellent factual information on type in its *A disagreeably facetious Type Glossary for the amusement and edification of people beginning a love affair with fonts.*

Well, they mean type faces, of course, but who are we to stand in the way of a little alliteration? At the time of going to press, you could find this at:

http://www.microsoft.com/typography/glossary/content.htm

If it is not still there when you read this book, please complain bitterly to Microsoft on behalf of all of us out here!

A brief history of type

A Brief History of Type, by Thomas W. Phinney. Phinney starts from Gutenberg and moves right on from there.

http://www.redsun.com/type/abriefhistoryoftype/

GLOSSARY

A

ascender
Part of letter projecting above the body or bowl as in b, d, h, for example.

ascending letters
Letters with a projection above the body, such as b, d, h, k, l, and t.

Axis of Orientation
An imaginary line at the left of a column which acts as a starting point for reading.

B

bastard measure
Text type in which the column width varies from the norm within an article. For example, bastard measure is used to accommodate a half column picture within the text.

The bastard measure accommodates the graphic.

black face or black letter
A type group which has straight thick and thin strokes meeting at acute angles, in imitation of priestly calligraphy. Some examples.

𝕺𝖑𝖉 𝕰𝖓𝖌𝖑𝖎𝖘𝖍 looks like this, 𝕲𝖔𝖚𝖉𝖞 𝕿𝖊𝖝𝖙 like this, and 𝕱𝖊𝖙𝖙𝖊 𝕱𝖗𝖆𝖐𝖙𝖚𝖗 looks like this.

body
1. Main part or all of a letter, for example, a, x or the rounded part of b.
2. The block of metal on which a single letter sat (figure 96, p.155).

body type
Small type set in blocks as text for continuous reading.

body text, body copy, body matter
The text of an article or advertisement, as opposed to the headline.

bold, extra bold, black, heavy
Type of normal form and size but with heavier strokes. Designations vary — typefaces may have demi-bold (half bold), bold, extra bold, black, heavy and even ultra!

This is Goudy Bold.

This is Goudy Extra Bold.

This is Goudy Heavyface.

bowl
Rounded, hollow part of a letter, for example, c, e, o, b, p.

capital
LARGER LETTERS, often called upper case letters, used as initial letters or in headlines — hence the word capital. (Caput is Latin for head.)

chroma
Purity of colors, in particular, the freedom of colors from white or black admixtures which take away their strong edge. Examples of high chroma are hot red, lime green, yellow and cyan. Adding white to colors makes them light, examples are pastels, while adding black makes them darker and dull, examples are olive green, gray, and black.

circular line screen
A decorative screen in which a photograph or art image is contained in concentric circles, giving a telescopic or target effect.

cold set press
A printing press which uses no heat to dry the ink. Material printed cold set is more susceptible to smudging than if heat is applied during the printing process to dry the ink instantaneously.

comprehensibility
The intrinsic nature of the printed word which permits it to be read and understood, to the extent that the reader may take action on any message it contains.

comprehension
The ability to read text and understand it to such an extent as to be able, if appropriate, to take action on any messages it contains.

condensed
Type of normal form and height, but with letters narrower than normal. Many types are designed with a condensed form, and some have extra or ultra condensed forms.

This is normal (or regular), Helvetica.
This is Helvetica Condensed (about 70% the width).

cursive
Typefaces that imitate handwriting. Also known as script.

This is a cursive typeface (Commercial Script).

This is another (Bradley Hand).

D

deck
A single line of a heading which has two or more lines.

decorative type
Type with decorative elements added.

Examples say it all. This is Champagne Script

EXAMPLES SAY IT ALL. THIS IS DECORATURA!

descender
Part of a letter which projects below the body or bowl, for example, as in p, q, y.

descending letters
Letters with a projection below the body or bowl, such as g, j, p, q, and y.

display
Arrangement of typographical and design elements to make printed material attractive to the reader. Also 'display type', often caps only, made for display use.

drop capital (drop cap) or drop initial

THIS is an example of a drop cap, a capital letter used to begin an article or section of an article, as in this paragraph. It may be two or more times as big as the body type, and may be inset into the beginning of the first two, three or more lines. When a drop initial is used, the first word of the text may be set in capitals.

E

editorial

In magazines and newspapers, text of news or feature articles as opposed to advertising matter.

eight on nine point or 8/9pt or 8/9

A type size common in newspaper and magazine setting, which denotes a type that is eight points, or approximately ⅑ of an inch high (but this varies from typeface to typeface), set on a body of nine points, or ⁹⁄₇₂ of an inch high, thus providing a small inbuilt interlinear space.

em, en

Measurements of type and space width roughly equivalent to the widths of the letters 'm' and 'n'. (See pages 156 & 157.)

extended or expanded

Type which has the same form and height as, but is wider than, the normal face.

This is regular (or roman, book, etc.) type.

This is extended in the same family and size.

F

face

A particular type. Corona, Futura, Optima, Helvetica and Times are all faces.

fix

A point at which material being scanned attracts the reader's eyes.

font (US) or fount (UK)

All characters in a particular style of a face, for example, Corona Medium Italic, is a font (US) or fount (UK). In handset days, font specification also included type size. Since type size is variable in computer systems, it is no longer included.

footer

Information or graphics appearing at the foot of pages, perhaps page numbers and title information, often an alternative to a header. (See also "header".)

G

gloss

The shine on paper often used for magazines or pamphlets. It may be chemically applied during paper manufacture, when it is known as coated paper, or it may be applied mechanically after paper manufacture by squeezing the paper between heavy steel rollers, when it is known as calendered paper. Coated paper is generally shinier and may provide more reading difficulty than calendered paper or matt/matte paper.

greek
Type placeholders used by designers as a simulation of text to indicate positioning and general appearance. Desktop publishing programs use gray lines of appropriate thickness to simulate type below a certain size which cannot be correctly displayed. It also means nonsense type which, paradoxically, is usually pseudo Latin — Lorem Ipsum!

Gutenberg Diagram
Devised by Professor Edmund Arnold and named in honor of the fifteenth century German inventor of movable type, this diagram shows how a reader approaches and reads a page of printed material. (See figure 8, p.30.)

H

headline
Display line at the top of an article introducing the subject matter.

header/running head/folio
Material appearing regularly at the top of pages, for example, the page number, book title and section title in this book. (See also "footer".)

horizontal line screen
A decorative screen in which the photograph or art image is contained in horizontal lines, giving the effect of looking at the picture through Venetian blinds.

hot metal
All metallic printing material, including type and illustration blocks, as opposed to photographic or computer-created material.

humanist
Sans serif typefaces based on the proportions of inscriptional roman lettering. Humanist faces, such as Optima, Pascal, and Gill Sans, have some variation between thick and thin strokes, which sans serif faces generally lack.

This is Optima, a humanist face, in bold form.

I

italic
Roman type style that slants to the right, *as in this phrase*. The term italic should be reserved for Roman faces; other faces that slant to the right should be called oblique. In the case of roman faces, the italic version of a face usually is more than just a slanted version of the roman — it may be a different design in detail or in its entirety. Note the difference in letter forms in the examples below. Obliques (usually used in relation to sans serif faces) are really just the standard face slanted.

abcdefghijklmnopqrstuvwxyzABCDEFGHIJ…
abcdefghijklmnopqrstuvwxyzABCDEFGHIJ…

J

jobbing or job printing
The commercial printing of leaflets, pamphlets, mailers, newsletters, cards, or inserts for magazines or newspapers.

jump

Continuation of an article on a later page or pages. This occurs occasionally in newspapers, but most frequently in magazines, where readers often are subjected to several pages at the rear which contain the spillage from articles displayed earlier in the magazine.

justified type

Type set so that both the left and right margins are straight as the body matter has been set in this book. (See also "ragged left", "ragged right", "centered".)

K

kerned type

The process in which letter spacing is reduced, usually between a pair of letters to produce better 'optical spacing' — spacing as it appears to the eye. (An overall reduction or increase in letter spacing to a large amount of type is generally called tracking.)

This type is set natural, without kerning.

Type set With Appropriate Kerning.

(*In 'Type', the 'y' snuggles under the overhang of the 'T'; the 'e' in kerning has been moved a little into the hollow in the 'K', the 'i' in 'With' has been closed up to the 'W' and the first 'p' in 'Appropriate' has been closed up a little to the initial 'A'.*)

kicker

One or a few lines, usually immediately below the headline, adding further information about the contents of the article.

L

light face

Letter of normal form and size, but with reduced stroke width.

This is the normal (or regular) Helvetica.

This is Helvetica Light.

light roman

A roman serif face with normal form and size but with a reduced stroke width.

lower case

The smaller letters, such as are used in text. Apart from the initial capitals (or upper case), you are reading lower case now. The term comes from the early period of handset and metal or wooden type: the compositor (typesetter) had two cases of type, the lower case contained the little letters and the upper case the capitals.

M

matt/matte

Dull or unglazed finish on paper. Most newsprint and book papers are matte. Office papers are matt. Magazine papers generally are glossy.

medium face

This may mean many things, ranging from the standard intensity for the type face to one step heavier than the standard, roman, book or regular. The body type in this book is Goudy Old Style, which offers no medium; the headings are in Eras, which offers weights of light, book, medium, demi-bold, bold, and ultrabold.

This is Eras Book.

This is Eras medium.

mezzo screen
A decorative screen in which the image is contained in large irregular dots, producing a crayon or pastel effect.

minus spacing
The measure of electronically reducing interletter space from the natural setting (i.e. the spacing set by the type designer). When it is applied overall to a paragraph or a larger body of type it is referred to as *tight tracking*, when applied to two or a small number of letters is it spoken of as *kerning*.

This type is set natural.

Minus spacing can even make letters overlap.

modern (style)
Roman typefaces with severe contrast between thick and thin strokes and with thin horizontals and serifs, often without brackets linking them to the strokes. Called modern, this style actually developed in the 18th century. Another name is Didone. (See "Old Style".)

This is Bernhard Modern, a modern typeface.

This is Nofret Medium, another example.

monospaced type
Mono = single. Type with fixed spacing between letters. Typewriters themselves, and the fonts which mimic them, are monospaced. (See also "proportional type".)

This is Monaco, a monospaced type.

This is Courier. Note how much space there is around the 'i', for example.

multi-deck heading
Headline that has several lines, usually more than three.

N

natural type or set natural
Type set in its natural form as designated by the designer, without interletter space reduction or expansion.

O

oblique
Only serif types that lean to the right are italic. *Sans serif right leaning type and similar faces should be called oblique* (although sometimes designated 'italic', nevertheless). Type that leans to the left is usually called backslant. The author prefers to use the term "deformed".

This is Futura Regular.

This is Futura Oblique.

old style or old face

Roman faces in which the serifs are bracketed to the vertical or horizontal strokes, and with minimal variation in thickness between horizontals and verticals. (See "modern".)

This is a type of the "old face" style.

P

PDF

Portable Document Format, a refinement and simplification of PostScript (see p. 160).

photocomposition

Type set by photographic means, as opposed to mechanical (hot metal) means.

photomechanical transfer

These used to be known as PMTs, until the initials became more widely known to denote a medical condition. A photomechanical transfer is a black and white photographic reproduction of a page of type and display images. They are sometimes known as bromide proofs. (A common trade name is Velox.)

pica

A printer's unit of measurement, equal to twelve points (see 'point' below). Six traditional picas are a fraction shorter than one inch (2.54 cm) but in the Postscript (computer language) measure, exactly equal to one inch or seventy two Postscript points. Pica was also formerly used to denote 12 point type.

PMS

PMS is the Pantone Matching System, an internationally recognized system of denoting printing colors. The system provides accurate proportions of inks required to make a specific color, which is then given a PMS number. For example, PMS 259 is a deep purple and PMS 286 is French blue. There are other color matching systems — Munsell and Toyo are two examples.

point

The basic unit of measurement in printing, $\frac{1}{72}$ of an inch (see p.157).

This is 8 point type.

This is 18 point type.

PostScript®

The computer language used to describe pages and their contents for the output device such as a laser printer or imagesetter (see p.160).

Primary Optical Area

In Edmund Arnold's Gutenberg Diagram (figure 8, p.30), the Primary Optical Area (POA) is the point at which the reader's eyes enter, or are attracted into, a page. It is, or should be, the top left corner of a page, or of a type area.

process colors

High speed multi-impression printing uses three ink colors (plus black), which are called the process colors. They are cyan (blue), yellow (lemon), and magenta (red). Each color is printed on one plate, the impression from which is superimposed on the other three to give the effect of full-color printing. Process colors can be used on any press, but are the standard form for web presses, which generally have the capacity to print four colors only on continuous reeled paper.

proportional type
Type in which the spacing around the letters varies according to the width and shape of individual letters. Most type is proportional. (See also "monospaced type".)

R

ragged left
Type setting in which the left margin is uneven and the right margin is straight as here. This is also known as setting right. This style is sometimes used in advertising material.

ragged right
Type setting in which the right margin is uneven as in this paragraph. It was developed to eliminate the need, in book setting, for uneven spacing between letters and words and hyphenated word breaks needed to attain the even right margin of a fully justified setting. However, there was and is no research-based substantiation for the idea that ragged right in fact makes for easier reading; in fact, the research points the other way — a good fully justified setting is best.

readable, readability, reading
Where these terms are used, the secondary definition (in the Shorter Oxford Dictionary) is implied: capable of being read with pleasure or interest, usually of a literary work; agreeable or attractive in style. What is not implied is the primary definition, which makes readable synonymous with legible.

reverse
Type set white on black, or on a colored (usually dark) background.

Reversed type, white on black!

roman
The foundation font vertical type style with serifs and variation of thickness in strokes, including curved strokes.

This book is printed in a roman face (Goudy).

S

sans serif
Type style without serifs, and usually with minimal or no variation in thickness of strokes.

This is a sans serif typeface (Gill).

script
A type that imitates handwriting. Also known as cursive.

serif
The small tick-like stroke at the end of the main stroke of a letter. The origin of the word is obscure, but may be from the Dutch word *schreef*, a stroke. Serifs were used in roman inscriptional writing as a means of finishing off the lapidary work.

Some serifs are straight.

Most serifs appear sculptured.

shade
A color value achieved by adding black to a color (see tint).

spot color
A single color used as a display feature.

style
Variation in the appearance of a type faces. Roman, regular, book, italic, oblique, medium, light, semi-bold, demi, bold, black, ultra, condensed, expanded and combinations of these and other terms are styles of various faces. The complete alphabet set, plus figures, punctuation and special characters in one face and style comprises a font.

T

Terminal Anchor
A device used to indicate to the reader that the article has ended.

tint
A color value achieved by adding white to a color (see shade) or printing a screen of the color at less than one hundred per cent.

U

unjustified text
Text set so it does *not* have regular edges at both left and right margins.

upper case
CAPITAL LETTERS (see lower case).

W

widow/orphan
Two schools of thought offer varying definitions of a widow and an ophan, although both agree that the main criterion is a line, usually less than the full measure, which is separated from the rest of a paragraph by a column or page break. One school says a widow appears at the foot of a column or page; the other says that a widow is the last line of a paragraph (particularly a short line, less than half measure) which appears as the first line of a column or page, and an orphan is the first line of a paragraph which appears as the last line in a column or page. The author has grown up with the latter definition, and is unshakable!

X

x-height
The height in a typeface of the letter x, which is also the height of all median letters (those without ascending or descending strokes). The height of type is measured from the top of the ascender to the foot of the descender. The greater the x-height of the median letters (such as x), the greater the perceived height of the type and its inherent legibility and the greater the certainty of deciphering (the criterion for comprehension).

A type face with a large x-height (Bookman).

A typeface with a small x-height (New Yorker).

REFERENCES

Original references

This is a short list of books which Colin Wheildon found most interesting, informative and helpful when he was developing his research projects.

Arnold, Edmund C., *Arnold's Ancient Axioms*, Ragan Report Press, 1978.

Arnold, Edmund C, *Designing the Total Newspaper*, Harper and Row, New York, 1981.

Evans, Harold, *Newspaper Design*, Holt, Rinehart, Wilson, 1973.

McLean, Ruari, *Typography*, Thames and Hudson, 1973.

Moran, James, *Stanley Morison*, Lun Humphries, 1971.

Morison, Stanley, *First Principles of Typography*, Cambridge University Press, 1936.

The Art of Printing, Humphrey Milford, 1938.

The Typographic Arts, Past, Present and Future, James Thin, 1944.

Ogilvy, David, *Confessions of an Advertising Man*, Atheneum, 1963.

Ogilvy on Advertising, Crown Publishers, NY, 1983.

Rehe, Rolf, *Typography: how to make it most legible*, Design Research International, 1983.

Typography and Design for Newspapers, Design Research International, 1985.

Tinker, Miles A., *Legibility in Print*, Iowa State University Press, 1963.

Other references

The references for people with a vision disability have already been given.

For type faces, seek out this book:

Spiekermann Erik, Jürgen Siebert & Mai-Linh Thi Truong, *FontBook: Digital Typeface Compendium* (2nd Edition), FontShop International, 1998 — ISBN: 3-930023-02-4.

If you are seeking more books about type and layout, you might like to try this site:

http://www.typebooks.org/

A good basic reference on reading research is:

http://www.readingonline.org/research/eyemove.html

A wide range of material was accessed on the internet. Search on terms like "typography", "typography in print", "reading research", "printing" and so on. Sadly, you will find little publicly available research about type and layout for print, although some good work including online, is happening in relation to type and layout for screen presentation. The STARCH people do lots of research, of course, but that is proprietary information. If they ever publish anything, grab it!

An encouraging word

We urge you to read more widely and to become involved in research in this exciting field. As you read further, though, bear in mind the basic precepts of this book:

- There may be an inverse relationship between the attractiveness of a page at first glace and its ability to work as a good reading and selling or communication environment.
- If the message is in the words, then there is no excuse for making it difficult for readers to read.
- Research, research, research. Opinions without facts to back them up simply are *not good enough* when decisions are being made about communication that may decide the fate of nations — or even just the fate of products.

INDEX

'Hands on' consumer advertising like it simply hasn't been done before

Written and illustrated in the spirit of *Applying the Rules* in our acclaimed, industry leading, *Type & Layout*, and *Advertising for Success* in the newly launched *Success in Store (2nd ed)*, as the cover promises, *99 real world advertising ideas to kick start your business today* takes readers step by step through 99 real world advertising ideas to help build business. Writing with his customary enthusiasm and vigor, Geoffrey Heard analyzes scores of real world ads, extracts key concepts and shows how to adapt them to advertising other small to medium retail and other businesses. The primary focus is on print, but the book also examines key techniques in different media, and translates some ads/concepts to radio, television, direct mail and the internet.

Who hasn't dreamed of opening their own store? Here's a book about how to make that dream come true

Success in Store: How to start or buy a retail business, enjoy running it and make money (2nd ed) by Geoffrey Heard and Gordon Woolf is 256 pages of dream fulfilment. Both have hands-on experience of small and medium retail business and between them they present a lively book for the budding entrepreneur of any age who is getting into "do it now" mode — who wants to fulfil their dream, indulge their passion and make the jump into their own retail business. The authors combine their experience to provide hints, tips and outrageous ideas for a wide range of retailing — from convenience stores to funeral parlors. They talk of pathways to success but pull no punches about how tough those paths can be.

THE PUBLISHERS' BOOKSHELF_____

The definitive book for anyone aiming to be the next big thing in magazines

The fact that this is the 4th edition of Gordon Woolf's How to start and produce a Magazine or Newsletter, speaks for itself. The Midwest Book Review (USA) called this: "The best instructional guide for aspiring publishers of a magazine or newsletter available today…". This is not a DTP book; it is a new magazine publishing entrepreneur's handbook — the author pays particular attention to the business aspects of publishing. No income, no magazine!

DTP production…

Gordon Woolf's deep knowledge of PageMaker and his scripting abilities, are legendary in the commercial DTP world. Despite Pageaker having been superseded at v.7, it remains a significant workhorse in commercial publishing. In addition, much in this book has general DTP application. This is the culmination of several editions linked to different versions of PageMaker.

OTHER titles in the Worsley Press Publishing Bookshelf include *Publish your Book* (2nd ed) by Gordon Woolf and *Pathway to Publication* by Peggy Graham.

Visit our website, www.worsleypress.com, for information and excerpts from these books and to purchase direct from our webstore.

Printed in the United States
82929LV00003B/9-108/A